ON SECOND THOUGHTS

ON SECOND

JOHN DOUGLAS PRINGLE

THOUGHTS

AUSTRALIAN ESSAYS

 ANGUS AND ROBERTSON

Also by John Douglas Pringle

AUSTRALIAN ACCENT
AUSTRALIAN PAINTING TODAY

First published in 1971 by
ANGUS AND ROBERTSON (PUBLISHERS) PTY LTD
221 George Street, Sydney
2 Fisher Street, London
107 Elizabeth Street, Melbourne
111-13 Adelaide Street, Brisbane
89 Anson Road, Singapore

National Library of Australia
card number and ISBN 0 207 12321 7

Registered in Australia for transmission by post as a book
PRINTED IN AUSTRALIA BY HALSTEAD PRESS, SYDNEY

FOR CELIA

ACKNOWLEDGMENTS

"The Future of Australia" and "Politics: Australian Style" first appeared in the *Sunday Australian*, and "Advance Australia Square" in *Quadrant*. "Literary Migrants" is a very much expanded version of a similar article which appeared in *Quadrant*.

CONTENTS

PREFACE

In 1957 I wrote a book called *Australian Accent* which caused some stir at the time and may not be totally forgotten now. If it had any importance it was that it was one of the first attempts to look critically at contemporary urban Australia, as distinct from life in the outback, and that it stimulated many other writers, most of them Australians, to do the same thing more skilfully.

Since then there has been a steady stream of books about Australian "culture" and "civilization", most of them highly critical and some of them very good. Indeed I get some amusement now when I remember the storms of abuse provoked by what I considered my very mild comments and notice how today much fiercer attacks are accepted without causing any reaction and even with approval. Perhaps this is the best evidence of Australian maturity.

I cannot help feeling, however, that the passion for self-denigration, so noticeable among Australian intellectuals in recent years, has now gone too far. They are so busy denouncing the things they do not like about Australia that they are inclined to deny that Australia has any virtues at all. This is absurd. Judged by almost any standards, it seems to me, Australia is one of the sanest, healthiest and most democratic countries in the world, and if it cannot rival older nations in the quality of its art and literature, it is by no means the cultural desert that some critics like to imagine.

In writing this new collection of essays, therefore, I have

concentrated on those things in Australia which have given me pleasure. It is not a book *about* Australia at all. It completely ignores a great many important subjects, not because they do not interest me but simply because I do not feel that I have anything new or significant to add to them. Only two of the essays are political, and even they may be considered somewhat frivolous in tone.

I am aware, of course, that this deplorable complacency may be attributed by my readers to premature senility. Perhaps they are right. I hope, however, that some at least will see in it rather the resignation of a ticket-of-leave man who, after serving two terms in the colonies, has become reconciled to his adopted country.

THE FUTURE
OF AUSTRALIA

WHEN I wrote *Australian Accent* in 1957 I was in some doubt whether Australia had a future at all. In the second-last chapter I wrote as follows: "Australians are fortunate in many ways—fortunate in having a continent to themselves, fortunate in having a high standard of living, fortunate in having as yet no powerful nation close to their shores; but time is against them. They began too late. If, like the Americans, they had been granted another hundred or hundred and fifty years to develop in isolation before the world entered the atomic age and Asia awoke from its sleep, they might have become a powerful nation with a distinctive civilization. Now the prospects are less certain. Left alone, they will grow rapidly in wealth and power, but they are terribly dependent on the Western world either maintaining its superiority or reaching some permanent arrangement with the nations of Asia and Africa. And even that has its dangers. If, for instance, a world government were to be formed in forty or fifty years' time, it is at least possible that one of its first duties might be to divide the world's goods more fairly between the nations by allotting northern Australia and New Guinea to the surplus populations of China or India or Japan. It would be a very hard proposal to resist, and the objection that this would mean the

end of Australia as a white nation is one which would not
carry much weight with the peoples of Asia, Africa, Russia
or even, perhaps, of America."

Since then similar doubts have been expressed in a much
more sophisticated and persuasive form by Neil McInnes in
a paper to a seminar held in Melbourne in 1965 by the Association for Cultural Freedom. This paper was published in
Quadrant in September 1965, and seems to me, with the exception of Donald Horne's *The Lucky Country*, the most
brilliant and provocative essay on the future of Australia that
has been written during the last ten years.

Mr McInnes too has doubts about the future of Australia
as an independent nation, but for different reasons. He argues
that Australia always has been a province, first of Britain, now
of the United States; that "our dependence or subordination
or provincial situation—whatever you call it—is irretrievable
and is going to increase in the years ahead; that in the matter
of being provincial we haven't seen anything yet; that maybe
the heyday of Australian national independence (poor shadow
that it was) is behind us, with Banjo Paterson and Dr Evatt".
And he adds, in words very like my own, that "we have
arrived too late to become a self-governing nation. We have
missed the bus. We are destined to remain provincial. . . .
Nationalism today is the luxury of newly liberated territories,
like their temporary experiments in autarchy at the beginning of economic development; they cannot afford it and will
get over it. The season is not for nationalism but for empires
and trans-national entities like the union of Europe now
being effected or the Latin, South or Central American
federations that seem to offer the only hope of liberation
for those peoples from inept oligarchies allied with the
foreigner."

Mr McInnes gives cogent reasons for his view. These, he
says, lie in the new technology and the dynamism of the international corporation. In military matters this is already
obvious and widely accepted. Because of the fantastic development of missiles and nuclear power, true military power and
national independence are now the privilege of a very few
super-Powers. The smaller Powers are quite defenceless and
even the middle Powers can hardly hope to do more than

offer some useful addition to the resources of a coalition. To put it bluntly, only the United States could now protect Australia from an attack by a Great Power like Russia, China or Japan.

But Mr McInnes argues that people do not realize that the same thing is happening in the economic sphere. Already nearly a third of Australia's industrial capital is foreign owned. "Of the top 50 companies in this country 25 are foreign-controlled." (This was written in 1965: today the proportion is certainly not less.) "Ninety-five per cent of the motor-car industry, 97 per cent of the pharmaceuticals and toiletries, 95 per cent of petroleum refining and distributing, 83 per cent of oil exploration, three-quarters of bauxite and aluminium, three-quarters of iron ore (leaving out B.H.P.'s own captive supplies), at least 60 per cent of chemicals, and half of food (and this is increasing), motor parts and accessories, and lead-zinc-copper and mineral sands." Our dependence on foreign research and technology is increasing. Within a short time, "as we enter further into the new technological era, the percentage of economic decisions taken outside will approach nearer 100." Mr McInnes is not unduly depressed at this prospect. He believes that it will keep Australia prosperous and contented. The masses will not particularly mind and the educated middle classes will have opportunities of good jobs in foreign-owned corporations. But—and this is the rub—we shall remain hopelessly provincial without a national identity or culture of our own. Moreover, instead of being a province of the British Empire, where, after all, we belonged and had rights and were recognized, we shall be a province of an empire (the United States) in which we are and always will be aliens.

It might be thought that these arguments would have reinforced my own doubts of 1957. In fact, however, I now take a more optimistic view. I believe that both myself and Mr McInnes were wrong in some, though not all, respects and that the situation is more hopeful now than it seemed in 1957 or 1965. I believe that, at least so far as one can reasonably foresee (which is not very far—say thirty years at most) Australia will not merely survive as an independent nation but during that period will steadily increase in wealth, national self-confidence, and influence. And I see no reason why she should not also develop a national culture which, though still provincial in essence, will have the distinct and vigorous stamp of the best provincial cultures everywhere.

I will deal with my own errors first. It now seems to me that (like many other people) I exaggerated the political and military threat posed to Australia by the Asian nations. I had in mind, though I did not say it explicitly, Indonesia, then in the grip of Sukarno's imperialist ambitions, and China, which was revealing very marked expansionist tendencies. More serious still was the possibility of an alliance between these two nations or, rather, a take-over of Indonesia by China through a Communist revolution in Indonesia which would have neatly by-passed the anti-Communist nations of South-east Asia like Thailand and Malaysia. That this very nearly did happen in 1965 is, of course, a matter of history; but the Communist coup failed and, however much we may deplore the consequent massacre of Communist supporters, Indonesia today looks a much less threatening and less formidable Power. China too is much less alarming today than in 1957 in spite of her development of nuclear weapons. Preoccupation with the Cultural Revolution, fear of the Soviet Union, and a growing awareness of her technological and industrial backwardness when compared with Japan, let alone with the United States, seems to have induced a more cautious approach and a more sophisticated diplomacy among her leaders. I also accept that China's expansionist and aggressive aims were always exaggerated in Australia. Her "invasion" of Tibet, which had always been Chinese territory, was brutal but was not strictly aggression; it should be compared rather with West Pakistan's suppression of East Pakistan's claims for autonomy. As for China's invasion of India, Neville Maxwell* and others have demonstrated convincingly that it was not Chinese expansion but India's "forward policy" which brought about the war between these two countries.

Secondly, any kind of world government or regional federation of which Australia might possibly be a part seems even more remote today than it did in 1957. In the Pacific area at least I think that independent sovereign nations will con-

* *India's China War*, 1970.

tinue to be the rule, though naturally some will be allied with China, some with Japan and some with the United States. I accept Herman Kahn's* view that Japan will become the dominant Power in the Pacific area by the end of the century and that the United States, Japan and possibly Soviet Russia will co-operate tacitly, if not openly, to contain Chinese ambitions. A balance of power of this kind, though not without its dangers—what system is?—seems to me to be one in which Australia could play a modest, useful and independent role.

I must now deal with Mr McInnes's arguments, which are much harder to dispose of than my own. For a great deal of what he says is incontrovertible. During the next thirty years most of the important political, military and economic decisions that affect Australia will be made outside Australia, and there is little or nothing that we can do to prevent this. But I believe that he underrates two important factors. The first is the power of quite small nations to make their own decisions provided they are led by able and determined leaders who have the support of their people. A very good example of this is Egypt. Twenty years ago no nation could have seemed less independent, more humiliatingly subject or weaker both in national will and economic resources than Egypt. She had only just escaped from centuries of semi-colonial dependence on Turkey, France and Britain. British troops were still stationed in the Canal Zone. No one had ever imagined, let alone suggested, that Egypt might take over the control of the Suez Canal from the powerful international consortium that owned and ran it. Yet within a short period President Nasser got rid of the British, seized the Suez Canal, and defied the greatest Powers in the world to stop him. It may be argued that even now Egypt is not really independent; she has merely exchanged her dependence on Britain for dependence on Russia. But I do not think it can be denied that during the last twenty years Egypt has carried out an independent foreign policy and taken many decisions of the greatest importance both to herself and other nations. (That some of these decisions were disastrous does not affect the argument.)

* The Emerging Japanese Super-state: Challenge and Response, 1970.

My second point is that economic dependence on other richer nations still leaves very considerable areas for independent action (for instance, the whole field of social policy). Of course it imposes limits on independent action, but then there always have been limits for all except the world's most powerful nations—and even they have been limited by the fear of what other great Powers might do. In spite of the technological revolution and the rise of the great American international corporations, I do not really believe that, say, Sweden feels or is less independent than she was, say, in 1870 or 1770. Why then should Australia? Moreover, in the last resort there is nothing to prevent an independent nation from nationalizing an industry and expropriating a foreign-owned business. Many small nations (like Egypt) have done so. At the moment it is not very easy to imagine Australia doing this, but one cannot assume that this would never happen. Mr McInnes constantly stresses Australian dependence on foreign "good will". But are not these international corporations and foreign-owned businesses equally dependent on Australian good will? He would surely not suggest that the United States would go to war to prevent an Australian Government from nationalizing Mt Isa Mines or General Motors–Holden's.

There are other minor weaknesses in Neil McInnes's argument, some of them simply due to changes since he wrote it. The most extraordinary omission is any mention of Japan, which has already become Australia's most important trading partner and may become an even more dominating economic influence than the United States. Admittedly, few would think it an advantage to exchange colonial dependence on the United States for colonial dependence on Japan, but the very fact that there are now three economic giants with interests in Australia—the United States, Japan and Britain-in-Europe —may make it easier for Australia to avoid economic dependence on any one. Recent scientific and technological developments also put in question his assertion that Australia can never have a nuclear industry of its own or nuclear weapons of its own. Both now seem possible if we wish it.

There is, however, one conclusion which seems inescapable from Neil McInnes's arguments: the larger Australia's population, the more likely it is to enjoy a measure of independence. Power and independence are now very largely a factor of size. A larger population means a larger internal market for industry—the only condition that would allow Australian-owned industries to compete with the great international corporations. A larger population means surplus wealth for research and development, for higher education, for defence, and, I would add, for culture. Under the circumstances of today a very small population—and by this I would mean anything under twenty million—must almost guarantee colonial status. It is no use romantics pointing to the achievements of Fifth Century Athens or of Renaissance Florence. It is no use even comparing Australia with England in the reign of Queen Anne when England, with a population of about five million, had, in Trevelyan's phrase, "the recipe for genius". Conditions have changed since then. It is more relevant to point out, as Colin Clark did recently,* that the stakes are continually being raised. In 1670 a nation could be an important, if not a great, Power with a population of one million (cf. Sweden and the Netherlands). By 1770 the minimum was six million (Prussia); by 1870 it was thirty-one million (Britain); by 1970 it was a hundred million (Japan). "It is clear that the 'ante' required to enter the world power game is increasing rapidly, some three-fold or four-fold each century."

It may be argued, of course, that the greatest population Australia can hope to achieve by, say, the end of the century is not going to make much difference in this league. On present trends, if both the natural birthrate and the immigration rate remain approximately the same, Australia will have a population of twenty-three million in the year 2001. If the net intake of immigrants were increased to 150,000 a year, then the total population would be twenty-five million. Would it really make much difference if it were five million more or less? I think it would. It is not merely that even another five million must mean some gain in wealth and power, it is the difference of attitude implied. Those who are advocating either a curb on immigration or a complete halt

* "What makes a world power?", *The Sydney Morning Herald*, 19th February 1970.

B

are in fact arguing for a Little Australia which would be content to potter on for ever in its present colonial role. Those, like Donald Horne and myself, who argue for the maximum immigration rate compatible with economic sense, are at least standing for the concept of a Great Australia with wider horizons and nobler aims. We would like Australia to cut a figure in the world, to stand for something generous and good. It is extremely difficult to believe that we can do this with a population of thirteen million.

Only two arguments against continuing our immigration policy seem to me to deserve serious consideration. (Of course I accept the need to slow down the rate of immigration from time to time to stop inflation and to allow the States to catch up in providing the necessary schools, hospitals, and services.) The first of these is the simple argument that since the world as a whole is plainly becoming overpopulated, then Australia should play its part by restricting its own population. But this is surely carrying universal philanthropy too far. The world may be overpopulated, but Australia is not. By any standards it is plainly underpopulated. I cannot see how it will benefit the world to leave vast areas of fertile land uncultivated and rich resources undeveloped unless, of course, we are going to keep Australia as a kind of World Reserve Bank against some future demographic crisis. To do this, however, would once again be to accept a permanent colonial status. Nor do I think it makes political and strategic sense. Even if other countries in our part of the world were prepared to limit their population, which is by no means certain, this would simply mean that Australia would for ever be weak and vulnerable in an area in which the Japanese already have 100 million, the Indonesians 115 million, and the Chinese 700 million. This is not an acceptable handicap.

The second argument is slightly more plausible: it is based on the fashionable cry to preserve the "environment". Big populations, its proponents say, mean more pollution, more destruction of natural resources, more overcrowding and human degradation. But this, too, is surely nonsense. I shall have a good deal more to say on this subject later, for I too regard it as one of the very first tasks for Australia in the future to preserve the environment and improve the quality of life, but I do not believe that to do this it will be necessary to limit the population to near its present level. For, once again, Sydney and Melbourne may be overcrowded, but Australia is not. I agree that probably the most lunatic blunder that Australia is at present committing is to permit the unlimited growth of Sydney and Melbourne when all the evidence from the rest of the world suggests that enormous cities or urban conglomerations of five million and over are disastrous. But with proper planning there is plainly room for another dozen cities in Australia of between 500,000 and 1-million people which I would regard as the ideal limit. Personally I would not mind very much whether these cities are placed inland or on the coast: I see no real advantages in placing them inland if in fact, as seems to be the case, people prefer to live by the sea. There is certainly room for two more cities on the coast of New South Wales at, say, Jervis Bay and Coffs Harbour, while Queensland is at least looking in the right direction with the development of Gladstone, Rockhampton and Cairns. But one cannot correct Australia's abysmal failure to decentralize by simply stopping population growth altogether. That would be a classic example of cutting off your nose to spite your face.

If, then, we accept for the moment that our aim should be a Great Australia with a larger population, from where is this increase to come? From Europe only or from Asia or from both? I have no doubt that this remains the single most difficult question facing Australia in the next thirty years. I have never been able to side either with the extreme champions of a White Australia policy or with its extreme opponents. In my view a rigid application of the White Australia policy is both morally wrong and politically unwise. It is morally wrong to discriminate against citizens entirely on the grounds of colour and it is politically unwise to do so when you live in an area in which all your potential friends, neighbours, trading partners, and enemies are themselves coloured. The rigid application of the White Australia policy must stop, and indeed has stopped.

But at the same time I have never been able to agree with those who refuse to admit that there is a problem at all or that there are any risks in permitting large-scale Asian immigration. I do not think it sensible to ignore the many examples from other parts of the world of the extreme difficulty of creating a multi-racial society. The United States of America is, admittedly, an extreme case. The American Negroes did not go to America as free immigrants but as slaves dragged unwillingly from their homelands in Africa. No minority could possibly have a stronger grievance or a more tragic background. It would be quite unreasonable to draw any conclusions from the experience of the American Negroes; perhaps the Puerto Ricans are more relevant. But can one really ignore the very different examples of Great Britain, of Singapore and Malaysia, of Fiji and Canada, of Belgium, South Africa and Rhodesia? There are, of course, happier examples: one may derive some encouragement—though not perhaps very much—from Brazil and the West Indies. But there again conditions were very different. And finally is it prudent to deny or to ignore the strong evidence that the white Anglo-Saxon race has an inbuilt prejudice against colour, as white Australians have already demonstrated both against the Chinese and the Aborigines?

Nor do I think that the champions of open immigration always understand the nature of the risks involved. It is not simply a short-term risk of riots and persecution and ugly examples of race hatred. One can overcome these in time by a mixture of firm laws and education. It is the more serious risk that in the process the country itself may become ungovernable or so weakened by dissension that the nation's progress is halted. Some scientists tell us that *in the long run* a good racial mixture is of advantage to a nation. I willingly accept it. But *in the short run*—and I am a short runner myself—it is plainly an advantage for any nation to have a uniform and homogeneous population.

Moreover, to encourage any sizeable immigration from another country or countries inevitably changes the character of the nation. So long as Australia took virtually all her immigrants from Great Britain there was no problem: Australia remained British-Australian. With the wise decision to accept more immigrants from other European countries after the Second World War a new step was taken. This was simultaneously a decision, which some at least understood, to change the character of Australia. And this, of course, has happened. The arrival of European immigrants has already markedly changed the manners, method, habits, and culture of Australia and will do so more and more as time goes on. Most of us think that these changes are for the better, but—and this is the point I wish to make—they were calculable changes which (or at least I hope so) responsible men took into account.

But to admit, say, an equal number of immigrants from Asia would again change the character of Australia only in ways that are far less calculable. For frankly we do not know and cannot guess what would be the consequences of mixing Moslems and Buddhists with Christians, or Chinese and Malays and Fijians with Europeans. For these peoples are not only of a different colour from us, which should not matter, but of a different culture, religion and civilization, which should. Is it in fact possible to create a united, viable, governable nation out of such widely different sources?

In spite of all these doubts and difficulties I believe the time has come for a further modification of Australia's immigration policy. I think this not only because to continue our present policy seems to me morally wrong and politically unwise but because, skilfully managed, a wider immigration policy which brought more Asians to Australia might actually help to increase our feeling of national independence and free us from colonial dependence on either Britain or the United States. If we have a future at all it must be as a new Pacific nation which is distinct from America and Europe and Asia. But caution is plainly necessary. Largely it is a matter of numbers. Mr Lynch, the Minister for Immigration from 1970 to 1971, has told us that at present Australia is taking about 3,500 non-Europeans a year together with another 6,000 of mixed descent. In his book *The Next Australia* (1970) Donald Horne suggests that we should take 10,000 Asian immigrants a year. I would accept that figure. It would still be less than 10 per cent of the total number of immigrants and, of course, a minute proportion of the total population. If we kept this rate until the end of the century we would have only accepted 300,000, though of course we should have to add to that the number of their children and descendants. It seems to me absurd to suggest that we could not comfortably absorb that number. It might very well be possible to increase to 20,000 at the end of ten years.

What kind of immigrants should we take? At first I think the Government would be wise to continue its present policy of accepting only those applicants who seem likely, by education or technical skills or background, to settle down easily in Australia. Eventually this might be broadened to accept some unskilled workers from Papua–New Guinea and Fiji, two countries for which we have special responsibilities and obligations. There is also some historical evidence that Papuans, Melanesians, and Polynesians do mix easily with Europeans. It is perhaps unfortunate that we ever sent back those Islanders who, however dubious may have been the methods used to make them "volunteer" for work on the sugar fields of Queensland, undoubtedly would have liked to stay in Australia at the end of their period of indenture if only they had been allowed.

What other countries might provide suitable immigrants for Australia? I do not really see how, if we once abandon colour as an obstacle, we can then discriminate between those of different races. But the obvious sources are Hong Kong, Singapore, Malaysia, Indonesia, the Philippines and Japan. The Filipinos have a special claim in that they are Catholics and therefore more likely to fit into a Christian society, but all these peoples are ones who should "assimilate" fairly easily. One would be a little more hesitant about India, Pakistan and Ceylon, not because these peoples are inferior but because all three countries enjoy such a strongly marked culture of their own. However, plainly there would be suitable candidates in all three countries.

The final object in planning an immigration programme must surely be intermarriageability. The only multi-racial societies that can even remotely claim to be successful are those, like Brazil and the West Indies, where intermarriage is the rule rather than the exception. I suppose a ruthless dictator might even go so far as to permit only girls from one country and men from another to insure intermarriage immediately, but that is not a solution open to a civilized nation. We should not expect miracles from Asian immigrants any more than from European immigrants; for at least one and perhaps two generations they should be encouraged to live in their own communities which alone can give them the psychological security so necessary to men and women who have been uprooted from their own homes. But the ultimate hope must be that they will intermarry easily and readily with Europeans. For this reason I would feel less happy about the admission of Negroes either from America or Africa, though it is difficult to see how we can continue to bar all American Negroes while encouraging white Americans to come.

We—for I hope that I have taken at least some of my readers with me—have decided for a Great Australia against a Little Australia, for encouraging immigration against restricting it, for modifying the White Australia policy still further to admit at least ten thousand Asian immigrants a year. What else must Australia do to face the future as an independent nation? I accept Donald Horne's argument that sooner or later we must become a republic. I do not feel that this is quite so urgent a matter as he does, but I agree that it is intolerable that Australia, alone or almost alone among sovereign nations, should continue to have its Head of State living twelve thousand miles away in another country. Even if Australians understand this curious anachronism, no one else can. Sooner or later we must break our historic link with the British Crown. Since very few of us would wish to do this in a way that would cause a lasting breach with Britain, we should be looking ahead now for suitable excuses which the majority of Britains themselves would accept.

There are two possibilities which immediately occur; the first would be the break-up—surely inevitable—of the British Commonwealth of Nations probably as the result of a mass walk-out by its Asian and African members over some such issue as Rhodesia or South Africa. (In fact this has already nearly happened three times: at Suez, and over Rhodesia and the supply of arms to South Africa. The Indo-Pakistani war also brought the Commonwealth to the edge of dissolution.) It is, I suppose, conceivable that if that happened the three white Dominions—Canada, Australia and New Zealand— would continue tamely to retain their existing links with

Britain and to acknowledge the Queen as their Sovereign and Head of State. There are plainly many Australians who would in fact welcome this. But such a decision would look so eccentric and reactionary, so backward-looking and old-fashioned in the eyes of the world that Australia should reject it as impossible. In my view we should inform the British Government *now*, that, if the Commonwealth of Nations is in an obvious state of dissolution, then Australia will not feel bound by any previous understanding but will feel free to decide what action she should take.

The second possibility is that Britain, having entered the Common Market, begins negotiations with her partners to form a political as well as an economic union. This too seems inevitable, though no one can foretell when it will happen. Once again I suppose it is just conceivable that the ingenuity of statesmen might devise a formula which would enable Australia—and any other member of the Commonwealth who wished to do so—to preserve her constitutional links with the British Monarchy. But I am convinced that such an operation would be plainly so illogical and meaningless that it would be far better to cut the knot. Here too an Australian Government should warn the British Government that, in its view, membership of a European Federal Union and membership of the British Commonwealth of Nations are incompatible. I do not think that many British politicians would disagree. Mr Enoch Powell, whose intelligence and logical powers (though not all his political views) I admire, has already made it abundantly plain that in his opinion the British Commonwealth is meaningless and irrelevant and Australians should be regarded as foreigners just as much as Nigerians or Pakistanis.

Now we are getting on! We have an independent Australian republic which is deliberately, though cautiously, accepting the need to become a multi-racial society, a South Pacific nation which has no constitutional ties with any other. We are steadily getting richer thanks to our vast mineral resources and, even though those resources are still being mined and manufactured largely by foreign-owned corporations, our increasing wealth and numbers are enabling us to share in these technological developments and even, perhaps, to regain control of some of them. What then shall we do with our wealth and independence?

Here, I think, Australia is faced with a unique opportunity. It seems to me that, among the so-called Western nations at any rate, this century can be divided conveniently into three periods. The first period, from 1900 to the second world war, was devoted to a struggle for a better standard of living for all their people. That has almost everywhere been achieved, and Australia is now, and has always been, among the front-runners. We are undeniably an affluent society. The second period, from the end of the second world war until now, has been devoted to improving the services provided by the State —health, education, and all that we understand by welfare. Here Australia has tended to fall behind the most advanced countries like Britain, Sweden, and Germany, but not so far behind that we could not catch up by a determined effort. The third period, from now until the end of the century, will, I am sure, be devoted to improving what one may call the quality of life—to making sure that people live in clean, healthy and beautiful surroundings, that they shall have both abundant physical and intellectual recreation for their increasing leisure, that the environment—I'm sorry, but I cannot avoid that awkward word—may be preserved so far as possible, that man shall everywhere live in tune with nature. It is here, I think, that Australia has an opportunity to be a leader and to set an example to the rest of the world.

In this third and final task Australia starts with many advantages. It is a staggeringly beautiful country with a superb climate. It is still, in spite of some fearful and obvious blunders, relatively unspoiled. Our seas—though not our rivers— are unpolluted. Our countryside is so vast that even the most reckless and improvident grazing and tree-felling have left huge areas of forest and wilderness. More by luck than good judgement our industrial areas have been located in such a way that they have not created huge, satanic scars on the landscape like Clydeside or Lancashire or the Ruhr. Even our cities compare favourably with most of the cities of Europe and North America. They are not, of course, as beautiful as Rome or Paris or Leningrad—their architecture and town planning leave a great deal to be desired—but at least they are fairly clean and well provided with parks and open spaces. Sydney, which is the worst planned and the most congested, is saved by its superb harbour and waterways. It would be hard to find in the whole of Australia anything that could honestly be called a slum.

It would be shameful if we did not build on these advantages to create the best urban environment—again!—in the world. Perhaps the most urgent need is decentralization—to stop the growth of Sydney and Melbourne before it is too late. I know this is a difficult task, but I cannot accept that it is impossible or that governments and town planners should simply throw in their hands and accept the inevitability of vast conurbations of five million and more by the end of the century. I have already argued that the ideal would be to create new cities of between 500,000 and 1,000,000, either on the coast or in the few inland towns that seem to have some capacity for growth like Albury and Orange in New South Wales. But plainly this will not happen of its own accord or without massive investment either of private or public money. It is significant that the only examples where decentralization has been successful in the last fifty years are cities like Canberra, Wollongong, Port Elizabeth, and Gladstone where either governments or private industry have invested large sums of capital.

Better planning will be needed on both a national and a local level. I am not one of those who think that everything should be handed over to the Federal Government, but under our present absurd financial system the Federal Government will certainly have to provide more money both for the States and for local government. But the States seem to me in many ways more suitable instruments for town planning. (I cannot help noticing, for instance, how infinitely superior the work of the Government Architect of New South Wales has been to the work of the Commonwealth Department of Works in Canberra.)

Both the Federal and State Governments should act *now* to impose the strictest laws on pollution both by industry and private individuals instead of lagging behind the United States and Britain. It is true that our pollution is not so bad as in these countries, but here, surely, we should be setting the pace. I would like to see other countries sending politicians and experts to Australia to find out how pollution can be stopped and not, as usually happens, the other way round. I have already explained that I do not think that the prevention of pollution and the preservation of the countryside requires that we stop expanding our population and developing our resources. Indeed I believe that we shall need more wealth to afford the kind of stringent measures I advocate. It will take more money, not less, to deal more adequately with Sydney's sewage than by pumping it into the ocean. That money can come only from rates and taxes. But I believe that Australians, like other people, will have to accept some limitation on their private expenditure and the satisfaction of their private desires. The most obvious example is cars. Sooner or later, it seems to me—but the sooner the better—private cars must be banned from the centres of our cities. I think there is a good case for a higher tax on a second car and for some tax on a second house. I would stop absolutely uncontrolled building on our coastline. While I would like to see a new city at Coffs Harbour, I would stop all development between Coffs Harbour and Newcastle.

There is an urgent need for more national parks. It is a scandal that Australia has no really big national parks on the scale of those in North America or Africa. Our biggest park, the Kosciusko State Park in New South Wales, has 1,507,426 acres. The Yellowstone Park in the United States has 2,221,773 acres, Serengeti in Tanzania 3,840,000 acres and the Kruger National Park in South Africa 5,120,000 acres. It is a miserable comparison. Here again an opportunity is coming with the decline of some of our rural industries. It should soon be possible, without too great expense, to buy back large areas of grazing country in the west of Queensland and New South Wales. There is also an urgent need for a really large national park in the Northern Territory to preserve what is left of the unique animal and bird life there. To be effective, as New South Wales has discovered, national parks must be properly policed and administered. And once proclaimed they should be inviolate from mining and other development.

But I do not wish to go into the details of preservation. There are many better qualified experts than I am. What I wish to urge is that Australia should decide now that preservation and control of pollution shall be an absolute priority, that we shall be second to no other nation in these matters. The cost will be high but the rewards will be enormous. I am convinced that in fifty years time—fifty years during which the rest of the world, no matter how hard it tries, must inevitably become still more overcrowded—there will be no advantage so envied as clean air and water, space, and natural beauty. The most privileged people will not be the wealthy or the powerful but those who can swim and sail in clean seas, breathe clean air in their cities, see the splendour of the stars undimmed by smog, camp in unspoilt bush within a hundred miles of any capital city, and enjoy the native animals and birds in their natural surroundings. I see no reason why these privileged people should not be Australians.

So far I have, I hope, been strictly practical and realistic. But before I end this glimpse into the future I would like to reflect a little on what may pretentiously be called the life-style of Australia. Here I am more hopeful than many of my fellow-intellectuals for, unlike them, I see great merits in our existing way of life. I should not like my readers to think that I am now so senile that I can see nothing to criticize. I take back nothing of what I wrote in *Australian Accent*. Like Donald Horne I sometimes despair about our political leadership and wonder how, if ever, we shall produce an *élite* to match our opportunities. The Ugly Australian is still everywhere only too easily seen and heard. Yet I think that in the past ten years Australian intellectuals have become so obsessed with criticizing the faults of Australia that they have become entirely blind to its virtues. Some of their criticism is faintly absurd. In *The Next Australia* Donald Horne has written amusingly about the tendency to contrast everything in Australia unfavourably with "Overseas":

> Having constructed Overseas out of all the nations, one then picks the eyes out of them, so that by comparison Australia becomes the Country Without Qualities, the least of them all, the world's one non-nation. They write better Overseas; look at Dostoevsky. They paint better Overseas; look at Rembrandt. They cook better Overseas; look at the Chinese. They're more liberal; look at Denmark. They're better at social services; look

at Sweden. The Japanese can arrange flowers better than Australians; Filipinos are better at batik; Paraguayans are more musical. Does Australia have mosques as good as Pakistan's? Sauna baths as good as Finland's? If there is some way in which Australia seems better than most places—whether in a relaxed style between persons, or in growing wool—this becomes a fault because of its oddity. That's not what they do Overseas. The mineral boom was acceptable. They have those Overseas.

I would like to add to this by pointing out the inherent contradiction in so much of this criticism. Australian intellectuals are always demanding that Australia should be unique and develop an Australian national consciousness while in the very next breath—or in the very next leading article—complaining because we are not like Britain or Sweden or the United States. One cannot avoid the conclusion that Australian intellectuals want their country to be "different" and Australian but dislike nearly everything which makes it different and which other people recognize as Australian.

I am not one of these. I see much that is admirable in Australian society even as it is today. I like its genuine classlessness (in spite of great differences of wealth), its openness to talent, its basic common sense, its refusal to bow down to every intellectual fashion, its good nature and tolerance, the good temper which eases disputes even between employers and trade unions, or between police and demonstrators, the casual ease which governs human relations. I think the charge that Australians are obsessively conformist has been grossly exaggerated: what other country, for instance, has accepted the new hair-styles and clothes of the younger generation with so little fuss? It does not worry me that in so many spheres Australia always seems a few years behind Britain and America. When you see a train heading for an apparently inevitable crash, you do not worry because it is five minutes late at the station. So if you regard (as I do) a great many of the trends and fashions of Western civilization today as disastrous, you are only too glad if Australia lags a little behind There is always the chance that we may learn from the experience of others and avoid the follies and mistakes they have made. I enjoy what Geoffrey Lehmann once called "our sweet colonial innocence".

I do not share Donald Horne's obsessive anxiety that we have not yet acquired a strong national consciousness and identity. I am not even sure that it is true. But in any case I am prepared to leave many things to time. Culture, like a tree, grows slowly; you must leave it to the earth of Australia. If we preserve our independence and our humanity, the rest will be added unto us. Who knows, even now, what genius may be kicking in a cradle somewhere in Esperance or Broken Hill?

Yet a man cannot help having dreams. The Australia I would like to see—though of course I shall not be here to see it—would preserve many of the qualities I have mentioned. But it would add to them more rigorous intellectual standards and more conscious art in small things as well as big. (At present we can build an Opera House but not a café.) It would aim consciously at a life-style suited to the future; less competitive, less aggressive, less materialist. It would understand that a certain simplicity, even austerity, which our forefathers practised because they had no other choice, is in fact essential to the good life. Would it be absurd to suggest that we might try to create a new, contemporary, civilization which still has something of the attraction the first voyagers found in the South Sea Islands? Australia too is a South Sea Island washed by the same ocean that washes the shores of Samoa and Tahiti and Hawaii. We have a climate which, for most of the year, does not require elaborate barriers against nature: nature is something (as people are slowly beginning to find) that people can welcome into their towns and houses. I sometimes think that our children have already discovered this for themselves. Throughout the long summer they run barefoot and wearing the minimum of clothes. They find their chief pleasures in the sun and the sea and not in elaborate pleasures or organized games. The young people too, with their style of dress—or undress—their casual friendliness and contempt for material success, may have something to teach us. Perhaps, to use Charles Reich's phrase, "the greening of Australia" is happening here too.

Above all we must get over the notion that in future we shall be judged entirely by our wealth and power. That is out of date. Wealth will always be useful for without it many things are impossible. Power will always be necessary because without it we shall not survive. But in future Australia, like other nations, will be judged by the quality of life it provides for its citizens, for the arts it practises, the happiness it enjoys. And, surprising though it may seem, I believe that in this race Australia might even come first.

POLITICS:
AUSTRALIAN STYLE

SHORTLY after lunch on Sunday, 17th December 1967, the office—I was then editor of the *Sydney Morning Herald*—rang me at home to warn me that Harold Holt, the Prime Minister of Australia, had disappeared while swimming in the sea off Cheviot Beach, near Melbourne, Victoria. I hurried into the office, only pausing to ring some other members of the *Herald* staff, most of whom were naturally enjoying that summer weekend on the beach or in the garden. That day began for me, as for all journalists and certainly for all politicians, one of the most extraordinary and exciting months in Australian history.

I do not propose to recount the events that led to the election of Mr (then Senator) Gorton as leader of the Liberal Party and so Prime Minister of Australia on 9th January 1968. They have already been told, with incomparable skill, by Alan Reid in his book *The Power Struggle*, one of the best pieces of contemporary political history I have read. I agree with Alan Reid's account in almost every detail, though I think it is marred by a very slight prejudice in favour of Mr McMahon and against Mr McEwen throughout. For the most part, however, my own observations, necessarily more remote than his, confirm his judgement.

I wish merely to add a footnote of no importance, a single

day during that period which struck me at the time, and has remained in my memory since, as a peculiarly Australian occasion. To do so, however, I will have to remind readers briefly of the situation at that time. By the end of the year four men had announced themselves as candidates to succeed Mr Holt as leader of the Liberal Party and Prime Minister of Australia. They were Mr Hasluck, Senator Gorton, Mr Bury and Mr Sneddon. Mr Fairhall had by then decided not to stand, though he would undoubtedly have been a strong candidate, and Mr McMahon, the Deputy Leader of the Liberal Party and the Treasurer in Mr Holt's Government, had been "warned off" by Mr McEwen who had announced firmly that the Country Party, which he led, would not continue to serve in the Government coalition if Mr McMahon became Prime Minister.

Of the four candidates, Senator Gorton was by far the least known and the most interesting. Though he had held a number of minor posts in the Governments of Sir Robert Menzies and Mr Holt, he had never been a member of the House of Representatives and had consequently made little impression on the public. Journalists, politicians and public servants knew him as a forceful, forthright, headstrong personality, but few of them would then have considered him seriously as a contender for the highest office. I had met him several times during my year in Canberra—usually at diplomatic parties at which he was a constant attender—and had come to enjoy our brief conversations. He would stand there, a glass of whisky in one hand, his other arm round the prettiest girl in the room, a cheerful grin on his handsome-ugly face, invincibly Australian, but always amusing, original and refreshingly forthright after the other politicians and diplomats one had met.

In the few months before Harold Holt's death, however, Senator Gorton had made a new reputation for himself as Government Leader of the Senate. He proved himself to be an able debater who could think quickly on his feet, and a few Liberals had begun to think of him as at least a possible leader if anything happened to Mr Holt. The Government's stock was clearly falling while that of the Labor Party was rising under the leadership of the youthful Mr Whitlam.

c

Would the combative, vigorous Senator Gorton, perhaps, be the man to take on Mr Whitlam and put him in his place?

That, certainly, was the view of the three men—Dudley Erwin, the Chief Government Whip, Malcolm Fraser, then Minister for the Army, and Malcolm Scott, Government Whip in the Senate—who met in Mr Erwin's office on Monday, 18th December, the day after Mr Holt had disappeared, to decide what the party should do. It was these men (as Alan Reid tells) who persuaded Senator Gorton to stand for the leadership and who then organized his very able and successful campaign. To win, Senator Gorton—or any other candidate—had to secure a minimum of forty-one votes out of a total of fifty-nine Liberal members of the House of Representatives and twenty-two Liberal senators. From the outset Gorton's managers felt fairly sure of twenty-six; the remaining votes could be secured only by hard work and persuasion.

Senator Gorton's main support came from Victoria, his own State. He was weakest in New South Wales where Liberal members had a natural loyalty to Mr McMahon and Mr Bury —and a natural resentment of the Victorian "Establishment" which had dominated the Liberal Party for so long. It was essential, therefore, for the Gorton camp to improve their position in New South Wales. To do this they shrewdly picked on Mr Wentworth as their chief recruiting agent. Mr Wentworth had long been known as one of the ablest and most original of all Liberal back-benchers, though his occasional eccentricities and violent anti-Communism had not endeared him to more cautious men. He had been denied office first by Sir Robert Menzies and then by Mr Holt throughout his best and most creative years. He undoubtedly saw in Mr Gorton his last chance of becoming a Minister—as indeed it was. He also shared some of Mr Gorton's sympathy for the underdog, for Mr Wentworth, though an extreme right-winger in foreign policy, is something of a radical in domestic politics. Once he had made up his mind to support Senator Gorton, Mr Wentworth did not hesitate. He became his strongest, most open and most forceful advocate in New South Wales.

Here at last we come to my story. For Mr Wentworth invited Senator Gorton to stay with him at his house on Pittwater, some twenty-five miles north of Sydney, over the weekend of 30th and 31st December—the New Year holiday—so that he could, in the famous catch-phrase, "win friends and influence people". Most of these people, no doubt, were other Liberal members and senators and officials of the New South Wales Liberal Party organization, but it was also necessary to try to impress senior journalists and television executives. For Senator Gorton had realized, far more clearly than the other candidates, that, although the decision was entirely in the hands of the Liberal members and senators, half the battle would be won if they could first be persuaded that he had public support. He was, in Alan Reid's phrase, appealing to the people over the heads of the party. That was why I came to be invited with my wife to lunch and spend the afternoon at Mr Wentworth's house on Pittwater on Sunday, 31st December, the last day of the old year.

Mr Wentworth's house is not easy to find. One approaches it along a roughish road over a steep hill which falls down to Pittwater. The house, a pleasant, rambling building which seems to have changed its mind several times during the course of construction, stands on the edge of Pittwater, surrounded by splendid, tall spotted gums. It was a warm, sultry day, half sun and half cloud, so typical of Sydney's midsummer.

We found we were the only guests besides Senator and Mrs Gorton, who were sitting at one end of a very long room which ran along the whole front of the house and opened onto the garden. All of us were wearing the kind of easy, informal clothes one wears in a summer weekend. Mr Gorton, I remember, was wearing blue shorts and a shirt. He looked fit and tanned and considerably younger than his fifty-seven years. There was also a large white cockatoo in the room, a friendly bird which from time to time left its perch with a cheerful squawk and flew across the room on its broad, buoyant wings just skimming our heads. Like so many parrots, it seemed to have a sense of humour. I remember seeing Mr Gorton's thinning hair move slightly as the bird passed. It was all very relaxed.

We had a drink before lunch and soon began talking. I asked Mr Gorton all the obvious things I felt a journalist should ask—about his attitude to Rhodesia, his alleged row with the Ambassador from Ghana, his policy towards federalism and the States. He answered them simply and, I think, honestly. I will not try to recall his answers now, even if I could do so accurately, since most of the questions and answers are now either irrelevant or part of history. What impressed me more were Mr Gorton's curious personality and a certain dream-like quality about the whole occasion. We had lunch with wine at the other end of the long room and then went back to our comfortable chairs for coffee. After a time someone suggested a swim, and we all went down to the private little beach to bathe in the tepid Pittwater, which as so often in summer, tasted rather as if it were made up of one part rain-water, one part drain-water and only one part sea-water. We had another drink and lay on the beach, still talking, on a grey army blanket Mr Wentworth had brought down with him.

Every now and then the phone would ring and someone would answer it. Generally it was an anxious politician or a journalist urgently seeking an interview or an answer to a question. Mr Gorton answered them all politely. Through the warm, lazy, South Seas air of that summer afternoon one caught faint echoes of the intense struggle for power that was being waged throughout Australia. Then we would all have another swim or another drink and the realities evaporated. As I lay there I tried to imagine a similar situation in Britain or France or the United States. Would Mr Heath or Mr Maudling have spent an afternoon like this during the tense struggle for the Tory leadership? Would Mr Nixon have behaved like this while awaiting the call from the Republican Convention at Miami? I could not believe it.

There was also the fascinating puzzle of Mr Gorton's personality. He was plainly an ambitious man, tough, aggressive, perhaps even a bit of an adventurer. He was what our grandfathers would have called a "galloper", our fathers a "thruster" and our own generation might call a "goer". Yet there was also something disarmingly modest about him, as if he was not quite sure of himself. Indeed at one moment he put down his glass, grinned and said quietly: "D'you know, I sometimes wake up at night in a sweat and wonder whether

I really want this job. It's a bit frightening." I formed the impression that, in his own heart, he knew that he had not either the experience or the intellectual powers to be Prime Minister, yet could not resist the temptation to "give it a go".

Yet he was, and remained, immensely likeable. Never once on that afternoon did he lapse into the jargon or the evasions of other politicians. Never once did he assume that air of pompous authority which comes so easily to those who have served as Ministers in Government. Many of the things he said obviously sprang from a sincere and natural wish to serve his country and his countrymen. As we drove back to Sydney that evening I felt that here at last, perhaps, was a genuinely Australian Prime Minister who would bring to that office a genuinely Australian style of government. It was an exciting thought.

Did it work, then, this exercise in persuasion? Well, no. With reflection the bright image faded and doubts returned. After reporting my impressions to my Managing Director, Mr Angus McLachlan, we both decided that the *Herald* should support Mr Hasluck or Mr Bury. On Tuesday, 8th January, the day when the Liberal Party met in Canberra to elect a new leader, the *Herald* published this editorial:

> . . . The candidates are not lacking in ability. Indeed Mr Hasluck, Mr Bury and Senator Gorton are all exceptionally able men, though none has had an opportunity to test his powers of leadership in a wider sphere. Mr Hasluck's grasp of foreign policy is well known; Mr Bury's economic knowledge is unquestioned. Senator Gorton's views on both are less known and this slight element of uncertainty about his candidature is at once attractive and dangerous. It is fair to ask not only what the candidates stand for now but what they would be like after 12 months of power as Prime Minister. . . .
>
> . . . In Federal matters, Senator Gorton is an unabashed centralist. He believes that the Commonwealth should decide the priorities for national expenditure, especially in such matters as water-conservation, and should then assume responsibility for carrying them out. This is a perfectly respectable position but it ignores most of the difficulties which the States are now suffering in such important fields as health, education and transport. . . .

We believe, therefore, that the Liberals would do well to choose either Mr Hasluck or Mr Bury. Both have the qualities necessary to make a successful Prime Minister. It would be far from disastrous if the Liberals chose Senator Gorton, but it would be distinctly more hazardous. Passengers would then be advised to fasten their seat-belts. If the Liberals are looking for excitement, then Senator Gorton is their man. But if they want to preserve the coalition with the Country Party and co-operation between the Commonwealth and the States in the task of national development, then either Mr Hasluck or Mr Bury seems to be the wiser choice.

When I look back over my career as a journalist in two countries and remember what fearful bloomers I made, what appalling errors of judgement I committed to paper, it may perhaps be forgiven if I now quote one occasion when I was absolutely, 100 per cent, dead right!

THE OPERA HOUSE

SINCE I first came to Australia in 1952 few things have given me more pleasure or more anguish than Sydney's Opera House. I was in Sydney when Mr Cahill, the then Premier of New South Wales, announced in 1955 that an international competition would be held for the design. I was still here in January 1957 when Jörn Utzon's winning design was published, and was one of those who warmly applauded the choice. I was away in Britain during the construction of the first stage, but I was back in time to see the great shells rising slowly against the sky-line—"With how sad steps, O Moon, thou climb'st the skies!"—and to take part in the furious debates caused by Utzon's resignation in February 1966 and the Government's subsequent decision to alter the design of the interior. For seven years I lived oppo-site the Opera House on the other side of the Harbour and used to gaze at it each morning and evening in a mixture of agony and ecstasy. Indeed for a time I became so obsessed with its progress that I could tell at a glance, each day as I passed it on the ferry, what piece had been added to its com-plex bulk the day before.

Today, when it is certain that the Opera House will be completed in two years' time, and when I for one feel con-fident that not only will it be one of the most beautiful buildings to be built during my lifetime anywhere in the world but that it will also provide a magnificent centre for the arts in Sydney, it is possible to look back more calmly and dispassionately on the disputes which have surrounded it from the beginning and also to analyse in a little more detail its peculiar qualities and defects.

Looking back I think it is clear that many of the subsequent troubles were inherent in the conditions laid down for the competition by the Government of New South Wales. Very briefly it may be said that Mr Cahill, the Premier, wanted an Opera House, not because he was interested in opera or knew anything about it, but because he felt that an Opera House would give prestige to Sydney and lustre to his own Premiership. Rome, Vienna, Paris had opera houses, didn't they? Then Sydney should have one too. While there was a good deal of naivety in his attitude, he deserves the credit for making the decision to hold an international competition and to go ahead and build the winning design. Without Mr Cahill there would be no Opera House.

Sir Eugene Goossens, then resident conductor of the Sydney Symphony Orchestra, director of the State Conservatorium and Mr Cahill's chief adviser, was, of course, a much more sophisticated man. He recognized that what Sydney needed was a centre for all the performing arts, but I think it is fair to say that his chief interest was always to obtain a new and splendid concert hall for his orchestra instead of the acoustically inadequate and very uncomfortable Town Hall where it normally played. Eugene Goossens was also interested in opera, but had no illusions about the demand for opera in Sydney or about the cost and difficulty of maintaining an opera company in Australia. He must have recognized that there was an inherent conflict between his ideas and those of the Premier, but apparently came to the conclusion that this could be resolved by creating a dual purpose hall in which both opera and symphony concerts could be performed. At the time these dual purpose halls were very fashionable, especially in North America. San Francisco, Edmonton, Calgary and Montreal had all built or were building one, and Eugene Goossens had been impressed by what he had seen of the new Opera House in San Francisco. This was the first miscalculation.

When these conflicting ideas were fed into the bureaucratic machine they came out as a demand for two large halls, a major hall to seat between 3,000 and 3,500 persons, to be used for symphony concerts, large-scale opera, and ballet, and a minor hall or theatre to seat 1,200 persons, for drama, intimate opera, and chamber music. There were also to be a restaurant, meeting rooms, rehearsal rooms and administrative offices. It is not difficult to see now that these conditions presented great and perhaps insuperable problems to any designer. Even if a satisfactory dual purpose hall could be built, which had yet to be proved, a hall holding 3,500 is really too big for *any* opera, while a theatre holding 1,200 is too small for grand opera and too big for chamber music. The figure of 3,000–3,500 was fixed by the Australian Broadcasting Commission, which administered the Sydney Symphony Orchestra, for purely economic reasons.

A final error was made in calling the whole complex an Opera House, presumably to please Mr Cahill. This naturally gave the people of New South Wales the notion, which they have never been able to get rid of, that the primary purpose of the whole scheme was the performance of operas. The Australian Broadcasting Commission, on the other hand, was quietly certain that its primary purpose was to provide a concert hall for the Symphony Orchestra. Between those two obsessions the real purpose of the complex, to provide a centre for all the performing arts, was forgotten. The competition should have been for an arts centre, and a more attractive name could have been thought of later.

The next crisis came with the judging of the entries in the competition. The judges were all men of real, though unequal, distinction. They were the Finnish-American architect Eero Saarinen; the designer of London's Festival Hall, Dr J. L. (now Sir Leslie) Martin; the Professor of Architecture at Sydney University, Professor Henry Ingham Ashworth; and the New South Wales Government Architect, Cobden Parkes, the son of a famous Premier of New South Wales who was one of the founders of the Australian Federation. Obviously the most distinguished by far was Saarinen, the only one with an international reputation at that time, and it was plain that his choice would weigh heavily with the other judges.

It is not true, however, that Saarinen, who arrived after the others, walked gloomily round the "short list" of designs pinned up on the walls of the Art Gallery, and then picked Utzon's design from a pile of rejects. Utzon's design had already been singled out by the other judges as one of the best. It is probably true, however, that Saarinen, who had himself specialized in the construction of concrete shells in his own buildings, was attracted by this feature in Utzon's design—ironically, as it turned out, since Utzon was forced to abandon it. It is certain that Saarinen recognized, and the other judges agreed, that Utzon's design had both outstanding originality and aesthetic qualities and was in many ways far the best suited to the site.

The site, as everyone now knows, is a peninsula of land jutting out into the Harbour below the gardens of Government House. What Utzon realized better than any other competitor was that any building constructed on this site would be seen from all sides and even from above—for the hill slopes steeply up behind it to Macquarie Street. It was therefore necessary to design a building that would look equally well from every angle and not merely a handsome façade with a box behind it. Utzon designed the Opera House as if it were a piece of sculpture—a phrase he often used himself—which would be seen in the round.

Moreover his solution to the problem of the two halls, by putting them side by side on a slightly converging axis instead of back-to-back, made it far easier to provide for the entry and circulation of people and cars. He could use the same approach to both halls and separate the audiences as soon as they were inside. But there was one serious disadvantage to this solution which the judges either did not see or did not consider serious enough to disqualify it. (None of them, in fact, had ever designed a theatre.) The peninsula at Benelong Point was just wide enough to accommodate the two halls side-by-side but not wide enough to provide side stage areas or wings for handling scenery for either hall. This was a serious handicap which no ingenuity either by Utzon or his successors could possibly overcome. Once the design was

accepted it followed inevitably that both halls would be
functionally imperfect and that unorthodox methods would
have to be employed for changing scenery and for staging
operas and ballets. This in fact has happened. It is characteristic of the whole Opera House that it has been necessary to devise very complex and expensive solutions to what could have
been simple problems. This was the second miscalculation.

The next difficulty was how the shell roofs could be built.
There is no doubt that Utzon originally intended the shells
to be covered with a thin skin of self-supporting concrete—in
other words a true "shell" in the technical sense. He described
them as "light suspended shells" in an explanatory note
attached to his entry. To a layman it must always seem curious that Utzon had not made sure that this was possible before he submitted his design and even more curious that none
of the judges seems to have questioned its feasibility. In fact,
as is now well known, it proved impossible to construct the
roof in this way and Utzon was forced to design quite different shells which, though similar in outline, are carried on
massive concrete arches. This change altered the appearance
and "feeling" of the building and added enormously to the
cost. It also required radical alterations to the foundations,
though it is only fair to add that it was not Utzon's fault that
the first stage was begun before he had solved the problem
of the roofs. That was the third miscalculation.

Even if this had not been so, it is plain that the judges
could not possibly have chosen a more *expensive* building
even if that had been their intention. The enormous technical problems of constructing the Opera House at all, the
originality of the design, the absence of straight lines and
rectangles, all guaranteed that it would be the most costly
building since Blenheim and Versailles. It is just as well that
neither the Government of New South Wales nor the judges
nor, apparently, Utzon himself had any idea in 1957 of the
final cost, for otherwise it would never have been built. No
government in its senses would have accepted a design which
it knew in advance would cost over $80-million. Personally,
I cannot regret this since the ingenious device of paying for it
out of public lottery has made it relatively painless. But of
course the ever-escalating costs were a major factor in per-

suading Mr Askin's Government, which took office in 1965, that something must be done even if that something involved dismissing Utzon. To that extent it was a disaster and must be called the fourth miscalculation.

I do not intend to discuss in detail how Utzon solved the problem of building his shells or try to unravel the complicated story of his disputes with Ove Arup, the designing engineer. That has been done far better than I could do it in various technical journals and, for the layman, in John Yeomans's excellent book, *The Other Taj Mahal*. Nor am I qualified to discuss his methods and his preference of choosing one firm to build an experimental "mock-up" for each stage instead of calling for tenders from several firms, which was one of the things that caused the final breach. I wish instead to move on to 1965 by which time the first stage, the podium or base, had already been built and the second stage, the construction of the shell roofs, had been "solved" though not completed. It was then that a few people "in the know" heard that Utzon was having great difficulties in solving the problems involved in the third stage—the interior—and, in particular, in reconciling that fatal conflict caused by the original condition that the major hall should be used both for orchestral concerts and for opera.

The nub of this problem can be simply explained. In the first place, if you are required to design a hall for 3,000 or 3,500 people for symphony concerts, then it is obvious that when opera is produced in the same hall some of the audience are going to be a very long way from the stage. I have sat about half way back in the Palace of the Soviets in the Kremlin in Moscow, an auditorium designed to hold 5,000, and, though the line of sight was good, the figures on the stage seemed absurdly remote and diminutive. Moreover the classical method of overcoming this difficulty, by building tiers of galleries jutting over each other, was impossible for Utzon —even if it had been aesthetically acceptable—because of the steeply curving arches of his shells.

In the second place the acoustic requirements for opera and symphony concerts are different. A stage must have an empty loft above it in which to house the curtains, scenery and battens. This means that if an orchestra is placed on the stage a great deal of the sound rises into this loft and is lost. (In opera the orchestra is placed in a pit in front of the stage and the singers generally advance to the front of the stage to project their voices into the auditorium.) This can be overcome to some extent by building a demountable shell over the orchestra for concerts and then removing it for opera, but this solution is clumsy and has rarely proved satisfactory. It is useless for a choir or an organ.

Finally, it is usually held that concert halls and opera houses need different reverberation times—the time it takes for a note struck or sung on the stage to reach the back of the hall and die away. Because the sung or spoken word must have clarity, an opera house needs a short reverberation time, between 1 and 1·5 seconds. But orchestral music sounds better in a hall with a long reverberation time of from 1·8 to 2 seconds. Once again, it is exceedingly difficult to reconcile these two ideals in the same hall. Inevitably a compromise must be struck which is less than ideal for either.

We shall never know exactly how Utzon would finally have resolved this dilemma, for he was not given the opportunity to do so. (In fact it is exceedingly difficult to discover how far Utzon had got with any designs for the interior of the Opera House.) But the Australian Broadcasting Commission discovered by chance that he was looking for a solution by cutting down the seating in the major hall from 3,000–3,500 to 2,800. Moreover it was said that he could only allow for this number either by putting some of the audience behind the stage, which was unacceptable to the A.B.C., or by placing the seats much closer together with a space between them that is permitted in Europe but would have been unacceptable to the Chief Secretary of New South Wales. Either solution was obviously far from ideal, and the A.B.C. promptly dug its heels in.

This was not the cause of Utzon's breach with the Government. Indeed it was only fully revealed after he had resigned. But it was symptomatic of the total lack of confidence and liaison between the architect, Jörn Utzon, and the client, the Government of New South Wales. The Government had appointed an Opera House Trust to act as its agent in all matters concerning the construction, but this Trust had failed to do its job. Utzon was certainly an arrogant and secretive man who preferred to make his own decisions, but there was in any case no efficient body with whom he could discuss the problems as they arose or who could tell him definitely what the requirements were. If there had been it is impossible not to believe that the problem of the major hall would have been argued out long before. If it had been, then I think Utzon would have had to tell the Government, as his successor Peter Hall eventually did tell it, that it was impossible to make the major hall a satisfactory dual purpose hall for both opera and orchestra concerts. The choice lay between a first-rate concert hall—and even that could seat only 2,800 people in comfort—and a first-rate opera house to seat not more than 2,000. It is plain that Utzon, who is a genius, could have designed either superbly, but even he could not do both. I will discuss which was the right decision later.

The argument over the major hall played only a minor part in Utzon's final breach with Mr Hughes, the Minister for Works, and the Government of New South Wales. The row was much more concerned with escalating costs, Utzon's methods of working, and inability to produce definite plans for stage three and the whole question of control. It is a sad and complicated story and I do not propose to try to unravel it here. Both men made mistakes. Utzon was foolish to resign in a huff over a quite trivial matter—his expenses. Hughes was less than generous in the terms he offered Utzon to return. History will inevitably back the creative artist against the politician and the bureaucrat—it always does in retrospect—though I do not think it can reasonably be denied that the Government had every right to be concerned at the lack of progress and the soaring costs.

The Government probably did as well as it could have in appointing Peter Hall, a comparatively young man, as design architect in Utzon's place, with Todd and Littlemore. Peter Hall certainly showed courage in accepting the post. Quite apart from the fact that there were still many enormous technical problems unsolved, he must have known that when the building was at last completed, any beauties and virtues it had would inevitably be attributed to Jörn Utzon and any faults or defects to Peter Hall. It is also to his credit that, behind the scenes, he continued to press for some reconciliation with Utzon which would permit him to return to the Opera House either as a partner or as architect in charge. It was not his fault that these efforts failed.

Peter Hall's first difficulty was, of course, what to do about the major hall. He first asked for and got a definite statement of requirements from the A.B.C., which whittled its original demand for 3,000–3,500 seats down to 2,800 but continued to insist that it should essentially be a concert hall with a reverberation time of at least two seconds. He then very sensibly went on a tour of the world to see whether any of the dual-purpose halls that had been built in Europe and America had in fact been successful. He decided that they had not. He then returned to Sydney and prepared the plan that the Government finally accepted. This involved abandoning the whole idea of using the major hall for opera; enlarging and altering the minor hall or theatre to make it suitable for opera and ballet as well as drama; and using the vast space beneath the stage of the major hall, which had been intended to house the stage machinery, to make a bigger rehearsal room for the orchestra and an additional theatre to hold 600.

Looking back today it is difficult to understand the storm of protest this proposal aroused. If one accepts, as I do, that a satisfactory dual purpose hall was impossible, then the only other solution was to make the major hall into an opera house to seat 2,000. This of course was attractive to opera fans, of whom I am one, but it would have meant that Sydney would then have two large theatres side by side and no concert hall at all. Could Sydney have supported enough opera and ballet to fill the major hall for twelve months a year? I do not think so. The champions of this solution also forget that while the major hall would have undoubtedly made a splendid opera house, more suitable than the minor hall for grand opera and ballet, it would still have been an imperfect opera house because of its lack of wing space. Moreover the A.B.C., though frequently irritating and unduly rigid in its demands, had a very strong argument on its side. The original conditions had listed the uses of the major hall in this order:

1. Symphony concerts (including organ music) and soloists
2. Large scale opera
3. Ballet and dance

and had added the rider: "The requirements above have been listed in the order of priority with respect to the attention which should be given to their specialized building needs. It is expected that ideal conditions will be provided as far as possible acoustically, visually and in connection with stage and orchestral facilities. Compromises which will prejudice the entirely satisfactory performance of a function with higher priority in the above list should not be made."

One can argue, of course, that this was a requirement inserted by one Government ten years before. It could be changed by another Government now. If the A.B.C. didn't like it, they could build another concert hall elsewhere. One is then inevitably drawn into the argument whether the development of music and musical taste in future will mean a demand for more concert halls or more opera houses. At present there is a good case for saying that both symphony concerts and grand operas are essentially out of date, relics of a nineteenth century bourgeois culture which are bound to disappear in time, but in that case one would not need a building of this kind at all. My own view is that we are moving to a point where the existing distinctions between opera and symphony concerts and drama will be blurred but that there will always be a need for large halls in which music, song and drama can be performed. But even if I am right, it still remains uncertain whether an old-fashioned opera house will be more suitable for such performances than a concert hall with a stage in the centre of the auditorium. Who knows?

Some of the fury expressed was undoubtedly due to the feeling that it was sacrilegious to tamper with the designs of the Master. People who take this view do not pause to ask whether Utzon himself might have preferred this solution if it had been open to him. Of course it meant removing the stage machinery from the major hall and so made Utzon's tallest shell, which would have risen over this, functionally meaningless. But, as I shall point out when I come to the aesthetics of the Opera House, the roof is far from functional in any case. Finally, much of the protest was simply the result of having called it an Opera House in the first place. Ill-informed people, who would never dream of going to an opera by Wagner or Verdi themselves, felt outraged that the famous Opera House would no longer be able to stage grand opera in the major hall. To them it seemed a monstrous betrayal. They refused to believe that the minor hall—partly because it was called "minor"—could be made into an excellent theatre for both opera and drama. Even those who should have known better flatly refused to believe this even when Peter Hall was able to show them the dimensions of the stage and orchestral pit.

In my own view the final solution was a sensible one though obviously imperfect. (Any solution would have been imperfect.) I am also convinced that Sydney will have a magnificent concert hall, an excellent though imperfect theatre for drama, opera and ballet, and a flexible small theatre for experimental plays. I cannot judge the interiors, which are not yet completed, but am encouraged by Peter Hall's elegant shapes for the glass walls, a technical feat not much less awesome than the construction of the concrete shells,* and by the light and beautiful ceiling which he has designed for the concert hall. It can be argued that this ceiling is rather too romantic in style to be wholly suited to Utzon's severe Gothic interior, but it can also be argued that Utzon's interior was a little too severe and simple for a hall that is, after all, designed for pleasure and entertainment. Sydney will have, what it most needed, an admirable centre for all the performing arts which functionally will stand comparison with any in the world and in situation and outlook will far surpass them.

Will Sydney also have a building of the highest architectural quality, to compare, let us say, with Canterbury Cathedral or St Mark's or the Tomb of Humayun or the High Court at Chandigarh? Let us reflect a moment on the aesthetic qualities and defects of this great building.

Two main artistic ideas emerge from Utzon's design for the Opera House. The first, as I have already noted, is that it

---

* I actually prefer Peter Hall's slender mullions to the very much more massive mullions proposed by Utzon. A prototype of the latter can still be seen.

D

should be a work of architectural sculpture, equally pleasing from every angle, a building to be seen in the round. The second was there should be a dramatic contrast between the massive podium or base, which Utzon took from the ruins of Inca temples which he had seen in Peru, and the roof shells which were to soar lightly above them, balanced like a ballerina on her points. The first thing to ask is how far these aims have been achieved in practice.

I do not honestly think that the Opera House is equally pleasing from every angle. That, perhaps, was an impossible ideal. It is best of all from a three-quarters angle when one can see all eight shells—or ten if one includes the restaurant, a touch of genius in itself—with the arc of one cutting into the circumference of another. Then the contrast between light and shade is enormously effective and the whole vast complex—and it is vast—moves and pivots as one walks about the streets of Sydney or travels over the waters of the Harbour. It has the life and movement of all great buildings.

It is slightly less effective when seen at right angles from either side and least effective of all when seen end on from the north or south. I have pondered for a long time why this is so and have come to the conclusion that the failure is inherent in Utzon's solution to the problem of building his shells. It was a brilliant inspiration to make every section of the shells part of the circumference of the same sphere for it enabled the rib segments to be cast from comparatively few moulds. And from most angles the spherical solution is very satisfying. But seen end-on there is something uncomfortable about the sight of two segments of the same sphere meeting at a point where they would intersect if continued. It has neither the logic of a Romanesque arch nor the balance of a Gothic arch. Indeed it is an arch which supports nothing but its own weight. I do not know if I am right in this supposition, but that is how it appears to me.

The flaw in the view from the side—say, from Dawes Point or Mrs Macquarie's Chair—is of a different kind and, perhaps, more fundamental. It is the failure to achieve that dramatic contrast between the solid base and the soaring shells which Utzon intended. The base is very impressive, huge, solid, austere, with few openings or windows or features of any kind. The shells are also marvellous and breathtaking shapes as they sweep up and forward—but they do not soar. This, of course, is due to the change in construction from genuine self-supporting shells of a light structure to ponderous shells carried by enormous concrete ribs. Some idea of what the Opera House might have looked like if Utzon's original idea had proved practicable was given in the sketch published in the newspapers when the award was announced. This, in fact, was drawn by A. N. Baldwinson, then senior lecturer in architecture at Sydney University, at the judges' request, as Utzon had not included a perspective drawing of this kind. But there is no doubt that it accurately reflected Utzon's design and was based carefully on the elevations and drawings which Utzon had provided. Those who bother to compare that drawing with the Opera House today will immediately notice a marked difference. The shells in the drawing were more romantic and more sharply curved. They *did* seem to float above the base like clouds. In the actual building the enormous thrust of the concrete ribs is evident even though they have been covered with gleaming tiles. The finished roof weighs some 26,800 tons—and, frankly, it looks it. Seen from the side there is a slight sense of strain, like a horse rearing on its haunches.

Yet the total effect is very beautiful. I like it best from across the Harbour at either Cremorne or Lavender Bay where the sense of strain is lost and the extraordinary subtlety of the total composition can be appreciated. It is splendid in any light, but best of all, perhaps, in the evening when the setting sun illuminates it from the west. Then the curves of the shells, echoing each other, look like huge waves breaking on the shore, each one poised as in the famous print by Hokusai.

It is admirably suited to its site. Many people have pointed out that the shells seem to echo the sails of the yachts on the Harbour, and the great glass walls on the Harbour side reflect the glitter of the water. The Opera House, like Love, "has something of the sea from which his mother came". The scale is admirable. The Harbour Bridge is a brutally dominating structure which might awe any architect who had to compete with it, yet the Opera House is never dwarfed by it or diminished. (In fact the top of the highest shell rises 221 feet above sea level and 25 feet above the roadway of the Bridge.) On the other hand one can understand Utzon's wish to demolish the tall buildings on the east side of Sydney Cove: they come a little too close for comfort. Yet the contrast between the swelling curves of the Opera House and the severe verticals of the city's new skyscrapers is very effective.

Close at hand one is more impressed by the vastness of the complex and by the perfection of detail. Utzon went to enormous trouble, for instance, to design the colour and pattern of the roof tiles so that they should be attractive at any distance. The whole design gains enormously from the immense steps and concourse in front of the entrance. These will look still better when, as will normally be the case, they are thronged with visitors and sightseers.

When I first saw the design I thought that the Opera House would be an exercise in contemporary baroque. Now that it is built it is strongly Gothic in character because of the great concrete ribs which support the shells. From inside these are very beautiful, austere and noble in style. Unfortunately they will not be visible from many places though there will be fascinating glimpses. This brings us to one of the central aesthetic controversies which surround the Opera House. Can the elaborate shells be justified at all on architectural grounds? I have never been convinced by those who argue that every feature of a good building should be functional. Is the spire of a Gothic cathedral functional? Yet one has to admit that the shells of the Opera House are a remarkable case of conspicuous consumption. It is true that Utzon intended the highest shells to cover the stage loft of both the major and minor halls—always a difficult problem for an architect—and it is not his fault that the major hall now has no stage loft to cover. Even so the other shells are purely decorative and ornamental. Moreover it has been necessary to suspend from these shells a quite separate ceiling, of considerable weight and thickness, to cover the concert hall and keep out the external noises which the shells themselves are perfectly designed to collect and amplify. The audience in either the concert hall or the theatre will be quite unaware of the huge shells towering above their heads.

THE OPERA HOUSE 43

Personally I do not object to this. After all, the interior dome which worshippers in St Paul's see from the nave is not the true dome. It is suspended from a brick and timber cone which in turn supports the outer dome made of timber and lead. Does this really affect the beauty of Wren's design? The parallel is a close one. I am prepared to admit, however, that if one thinks in functional terms, Utzon chose an extraordinarily expensive way to keep the rain out!

Yet, when all the possible criticisms have been made, has a nobler or more beautiful building been built in our lifetime? Would any other design have been so perfectly suited to its magnificent site or more in tune with Sydney's urban seascape? It is no accident, I think, that it has already replaced the Harbour Bridge as the symbol of Sydney in photographs and advertisements all over the world, and that its outline is familiar to hundreds and thousands of people who have never been to Sydney. There it stands, like Santa Maria della Salute on the lagoon in Venice, a perfect symbol linking the city to the sea, welcoming incoming ships with its wide open arches, shining brilliantly in the summer sun or gleaming palely by moonlight, contemporary in feeling yet reminding us of other ages when great buildings were built to the glory of God or the splendour of princes and not simply for utilitarian purposes. I believe it is a building of which all Australians may rightly be proud, perhaps the only true work of architecture on this continent. And I trust that, late as it is, some generous act of reconciliation and recognition will be made to the great Dane who designed it.

OF BIRDS AND POETS

To anyone coming to Australia for the first time one of the great surprises are Australian birds. Englishmen tend to be snobbish about their birds —as about so many other things. They are convinced that not only do they have more species of birds than anyone else, but that they are more varied, more beautiful and sing with more melodious notes. And indeed they have much to be proud of. Britain is a wet and fertile land which can support a very large number of birds to the square mile. Any fair-sized garden may boast twenty or thirty different species. It also has an astonishing range of scenery in a small space so that it is possible, without travelling too far, to see such different species as the golden eagle, curlew, and blackcock of the Scottish moors, the marsh harrier, bittern, and avocet of the Norfolk Broads, and the many seabirds of the West coast. And since many parts of Europe where Englishmen go for their holidays—though, of course not all—have relatively few birds, they are inclined to assume that in this respect, as in so many others, they have been uniquely blest by Nature!

I must confess that, perhaps unconsciously, I shared this prejudice on my first arrival in this country. How delightful to be disillusioned so soon! I can still remember vividly my first glimpse of the rich bird life which awaited me. The ship had stopped at Melbourne on its way to Sydney and a friend took us out for a drive into the Dandenongs—then less built up than now. We went a walk through the hills, marvelling at the tall eucalypts and enjoying for the first time the sounds and scents of the Australian bush. I heard a few birds which I could not identify, but, as so often in heavily forested country, these were not easy to see. On our way back we stopped at a café for tea. The café was not inviting. It had one dingy room with linoleum on the floor and fly-blown curtains. I felt slightly depressed. Suddenly I glanced out of the window on to a still more sordid cabbage-patch—and could not believe my eyes. There, feeding on the cabbage rows, were seven or eight of the most beautiful birds I had ever seen, each one a vivid splash of crimson, blue and green. They looked so exotic on that dingy background that they took my breath away. I knew, of course, that they were parrots but I did not know what species, and I had never imagined that parrots could be seen so near a great city and in such commonplace surroundings. They were, in fact, crimson rosellas, and in that moment I fell head over heels in love with the Australian bush and the beautiful birds that inhabit it.

Even now, twenty years later, it is still, perhaps, the parrots that astonish me most. I can never quite get over the feeling, born out of childhood visits to zoos in Britain, that parrots are rare and exotic creatures which can be seen only in tropical jungles among heavy purple and scarlet flowers. In fact about one-fifth of all the 316 species of parrots, cockatoos and allied birds live in Australia, and many of them are fairly common. Nor does the glory of their plumage have any relation to their background. The marvellous rosellas and lorikeets glow all the more vividly against the khaki, olive and soft greens of the coastal forests, while the galahs and white cockatoos can be seen in hundreds feeding on the seeds of the bare, inland plains. (Cockatoos, by the way, are larger than parrots. They tend to have short tails, broad round wings and a distinct crest. True parrots have long tails, narrow pointed wings and no crest.)

There are, of course, rarer species of parrots, and many of them I have not yet seen though I still hope to do so. But it seems churlish to grumble because one has not yet seen, say, the gorgeous king parrot, when almost every day one can see other species of almost equal beauty. Indeed I sometimes feel like stopping a passer-by in the streets of Sydney, seizing him by the lapels of his coat and shouting: "Do you realize that you can see, within a few miles of this city and with the minimum of effort, three of the most beautiful parrots in the world?" Both the crimson rosella and the eastern rosella are fairly common round Sydney, and both often invade suburban gardens on the North Shore. Every time I see an eastern rosella, a miracle of yellow, scarlet and blue when perched, but a flash of blue and green when flying, I am convinced that *it* is the most beautiful—until I see the next crimson rosella when I return to my old allegiance. And thousands of rainbow lorikeets, charming little birds with an almost ridiculously lavish allowance of colours, scream through the trees of Palm Beach and Pittwater, feeding on the flowers of the eucalypts. These have the added attraction that they are exceedingly easily tamed if you offer them their favourite food, which is honey. We feed them each evening on our balcony and, the moment they see me, they swoop down with a whirr of scarlet and green wings to perch on the rail until I place the dish for them, when they will hop down clumsily—because of the arrangement of their feet, with two claws forward and two backwards, parrots are marvellously agile in trees but on the ground walk like a drunken sailor—and lick up the honey with their brush-tipped tongues. They are enchanting birds, managing, like all parrots, to be both beautiful and slightly comic at the same time, and appear to have absolutely no fear of man. No matter how often I feed them I cannot get over the miracle of sitting on the balcony while seven or eight lorikeets feed at my feet and sometimes, out of idle curiosity, peck at my shoe laces. They are also superb flyers with their long narrow wings and tails, and at sunset it is a breathtaking sight to see flocks of them hurling themselves through the branches of the trees, twisting and turning, at what cannot be less than forty miles an hour.

The citizens of Canberra are even more fortunate. A Member of Parliament, leaving the House to walk to the Canberra Hotel, can see on any evening numerous crimson and eastern rosellas feeding with countless red-backed parrots on the

stately avenues of the capital. If he drives even a few miles
into the country he is bound to see white cockatoos and
galahs, and in the winter, when he goes to a diplomatic re-
ception in Mugga Way, he will see flocks of the noisy but
beautiful gang-gang parrots—really cockatoos—craning down
their rosy heads to peer at him while they scream their harsh,
sardonic cry from the gum-trees on each side of the road.
And if he cares about birds—which is perhaps improbable—
he can drive up into the thickly wooded ranges of Brindabella and glimpse, as I once did, a flock of the giant yellow-
tailed black cockatoos, looking almost as large as eagles as
they flap heavily through the big timber, calling harshly to
each other. In the dark, sombre gullies they seemed like
evil spirits or huge bats aroused from a tomb:

> the wild black cockatoos, tossed on the crest
> of their high trees, crying the world's unrest.

Nothing is more difficult than to describe a bird to someone
who has never seen or heard it. But here I am lucky. All the
poets of Australia seem to love birds and have described them
with a vividness and precision I could not hope to rival. I
propose to borrow from them shamelessly. Judith Wright,
from one of whose poems these lines are taken, is the richest
source: in 1962 she published a whole volume of poems on
birds. But there is hardly a contemporary Australian poet
who has not written at least two or three. I think of Judith
Wright as the poet of parrots and the birds of the forest;
of Douglas Stewart as the poet of the little finches, scarlet
robins, and honeyeaters; of David Campbell as the poet of the
hawks which hang motionless over the bare Monaro hills and
the "windy crows" whose harsh, melancholy cry is perhaps
the most unforgettable of all Australian bird-sounds. But
birds, like flowers and girls and words, are the poet's cur-
rency: I could fill an anthology with poems on the magpie
alone.

Far the commonest of Australia's cockatoos are the sulphur-
crested white cockatoos and the galahs. The galahs, especially,
can be seen in enormous numbers almost anywhere in the
inland; they are as common as wood pigeons in England—
and almost as unpopular with wheat farmers. Indeed because

they are so common they are not appreciated. Galahs are something of a joke to people in the country and, for some reason which I have never been able to understand, the word is used to describe any stupid or idiotic individual—"You silly galah!" But poets and writers have always been quick to recognize their beauty. Let me quote this description from Francis Ratcliffe's *Flying Fox and Drifting Sand*, one of the best books ever written about the Australian outback.

Galahs are lovely things. Their breasts and underparts are of varying shades of rich rose. Their backs and wings are bluish grey. Sometimes, when the light falls on them, this colour looks almost as pale as clean smoke—rather like the colour which the sky assumes when there is a haze on the horizon. At all times of the day galahs can be seen in twos and threes sailing about with their easy but unsteady flight, but it is in the evening that they provide their great spectacle. At the close of day they gather together in flocks, and fly about in mass formation like so many of the parrot tribe. And with every swift change of direction the birds take on a different hue. One moment they will be flying down the light, a cloud of grey ghosts barely visible against the eastern sky. Then in a flash they will wheel round towards the sun; and it seems for all the world as if a new flock had suddenly come into being, as though solid bird bodies had been created out of nothing but the thin air and the sunset colours.

And I cannot resist adding these lines from Judith Wright's poem, "For New Engand":

But look, oh look, the Gothic tree's on fire
with blown galahs, and fuming with wild wings.

As for the white cockatoo, it is familiar to nearly everyone as the most common of all tame parrots in cages, "That sulphur-crested bird with great white wings,/The wise, harsh bird—as old and wise as Time";* but no one who has not seen white cockatoos in the Australian bush can have any idea of their beauty. I remember in particular an evening near Jindabyne in the Snowy Mountains when a large flock of them came calling harshly across the river flat to roost in the

---

* From Rosemary Dobson's "Child with a Cockatoo".

branches of a dead gum-tree. And as the great birds settled, their white wings gleaming in the evening sun, it looked as though the old, dead tree had burst into life again and put out white roses on its withered branches.

Douglas Stewart describes a similar moment in a more striking image in his poem "White Cockatoo".

Now they have left the moon out over the paddock
That should have been shut in the dark with the sun for
    padlock
And pale like a ghost it floats where the blue noon burns.
Keep the night's creatures away! For see, it's escaping,
Whiter, enormous it flies at my red-gum flapping
In a flurry of snow with black legs reaching, and turns
To a great white cockatoo that, bird or no bird,
Shrieks in a voice that only night should have heard
And rears up its yellow crest as wild as the moon's.

By now it must be pretty obvious that I am not a professional ornithologist or even a professional bird-watcher. I do not rise before dawn to net and ring the little honeyeaters and finches. Nothing would induce me to camp all night in the sopping gullies of the rain-forest to catch a glimpse of the lyrebird or the great masked owl. I am content to keep my eyes open when I go about my ordinary business or sit in my garden in the evening—and it is surprising what you can see if only you are prepared to sit and watch. For such a lazy, unambitious bird-watcher, Australian birds have many advantages. A good many of them are fairly large, which, of course, makes them easier to see and recognize. Many of them are also surprisingly tame. Even the most uninterested householder can hardly help getting to know, for instance, the kookaburra, the magpie and the currawong, all of which practically insist on close acquaintance with human beings. All three are bold, aggressive birds—the Australian magpie and the currawong both belong to the shrike family, while the kookaburra is really a burly kingfisher—and will do almost anything for food. Kookaburras are especially bold. Not only will they take scraps readily from the hand but they will sometimes, literally, take the food out of your mouth. On several occasions my wife and I have been eating our lunch in the garden when a kookaburra has flown down and taken a piece of salami or meat from our fingers just as we were putting it between our lips. Since the kookaburra is a big, heavy bird about seventeen inches in length with a formidable beak, this is quite an alarming experience! One family of five kookaburras at our house on Pittwater became so demanding that we had to stop feeding them on the balcony. The moment we appeared they would arrive and sit in a row on the rail, glaring at us with their steely eyes, and sometimes even pecking at us when we passed. Tired of this bullying we made a birdtable for them—and other birds—at the side of the house and had no more trouble. This bird-table has a bath filled with water into which the kookaburras love to plunge bodily. Their splashing sometimes wakens us in the morning if we have not already been woken long before by their peals of mocking laughter, one of the most extraordinary of all birdcalls and one of the most characteristic sounds of the Australian bush. They are one of the very first birds to call each morning and the very last to call at night when the sun has set. Long after the currawongs and parrots are silent and one is already listening for the haunting, monotonous cry of the boobook owl, the peace is suddenly rent by wild, sobbing, hysterical laughter: the kookaburras are having their last laugh.

The magpies and currawongs are only slightly shyer and less aggressive. The magpie sometimes attacks human beings in defence of its nesting site. In spite of this habit they are friendly and endearing birds, easily tamed and rightly popular. Their lovely, melodious, yodelling cry is one of the most beautiful of all Australian bird-calls, heard especially in the dawn.

As I have already said, I could fill an anthology of poems about the magpie, but two stand out in my mind as the most vivid and accurate. The first is by James McAuley:

> The magpie's mood is never surly;
> Every morning, waking early,
> He gargles music in his throat.
> The liquid squabble of his note,

Its silver stridencies of sound,
The bright confusions and the round
Bell-cadences, are pealed
Over the frosty half-ploughed field.

Then swooping down self-confidently
From the fence-post or the tree,
He swaggers in pied feather coat
And slips the fat worms down his throat.

Now Judith Wright:

Along the road the magpies walk
with hands in pockets, left and right.
They tilt their heads, and stroll and talk.
In their well-fitted black and white

they look like certain gentlemen
who seem most nonchalant and wise
until their meal is served—and then
what clashing beaks, what greedy eyes!

But not one man that I have heard
throws back his head in such a song
of grace and praise—no man nor bird.
Their greed is brief; their joy is long.
For each is born with such a throat
as thanks his God with every note.

It seems to me that even an Eskimo who reads these two poems would know exactly what the magpie looks and sounds like!

The currawongs are less popular and have a bad reputation for bird-nesting and egg-robbing, but personally I cannot help liking this bold, elegant black and white bird with its long tail and bright golden eyes, and its ringing cries, "currawong, currawong", as it swoops and flits from tree to tree. I am glad that Judith Wright shares my feelings:

The currawong has shallow eyes—
bold shallow buttons of yellow glass
that see all round his sleek black skull.

Small birds sit quiet when he flies;
mothers of nestlings cry *Alas!*
He is a gangster, his wife's a moll.

But I remember long ago
(a child beside the seldom sea)
the currawongs as wild as night
quarrelling, talking, crying so,
in the scarlet-tufted coral-tree;
and past them that blue stretch of light,

the ocean with its dangerous song.
Robber then and robber still,
he cries now with the same strange word
(*currawong—currawong*)
that from those coxcomb trees I heard.
Take my bread and eat your fill,
bold, cruel and melodious bird.

It has often been said that Australian birds are unmusical
and have no true song. This is a gross libel, though it conceals
a genuine difference from British birds. Britain has many
songsters, like the blackbird, thrush, blackcap, and other
warblers, not to mention the nightingale, which do whistle
or trill recognizable melodies. To listen to them is, in a sense,
like listening to classical music. Australian bird-song, on the
other hand, is made up of innumerable calls and cries, some
strange and bizarre, others soft and melodious, which, if you
are prepared to open your ears to a new experience, are no
less beautiful. But it is like listening to the contemporary
music, say, of Messiaen or Boulez after listening to Schubert
and Mozart. To sit in the bush and hear the ringing notes of
the currawongs, the whistle and crack of the whipbird and the
amazing variety of whistles and cries of the parrots, wattle-
birds, cuckoos, and honeyeaters is to me as wonderful as to
wake up in southern England to the dawn chorus of black-
birds and thrushes.

Moreover Australia has some birds which sing a pure
melody that can rival any English bird. I have already mentioned the curious yodelling call of the magpie. A closely
related bird, the grey shrike or butcherbird, is even more
beautiful. The butcherbird reminds me a little of the well-
known Australian tenor, Donald Smith. Stolid, stocky, plain-

coloured, uncompromisingly Australian, with a slightly hooked beak, it stands boldly on a branch, as Donald Smith stands on the stage, the last creature one might connect with song and music. Then it opens its bill wide and pours out an incredible stream of notes in a pure, contralto voice. At times it can sound exactly like a virtuoso flautist, and the variety and invention of its grace-notes are staggering. It also has the agreeable and unusual characteristic of singing more and better as the year goes on until in autumn, when other birds tend to fall silent, it reaches the perfection of its art. I would be prepared to back the butcherbird against the nightingale in an ornithological Singspiel or Eisteddfod!

There are, of course, many small Australian birds of equal interest and beauty which are hard to see. The many species of honeyeater, in particular, are maddeningly difficult both to see and identify. Most of them find their food in the branches of the eucalypts and they seem to have a special knack of always keeping at least two gum-leaves between them and the watcher with his field-glasses. They are also always on the move, slipping from branch to branch, so that they will not stay long enough in one spot to see them properly. The same thing is true of the tiny jewel-like pardalotes and the silvereyes. But the lovely little finches—my favourites are the diamond firetail and red-browed finch—are both fairly common and fairly easy to see, and the marvellous bluewrens, tiny, delicate birds with brilliant blue enamelled on the heads, breasts and backs of the male birds, can be found in every suburban garden. Douglas Stewart shares my love for the little finches. He has written two separate poems on the firetails; after much hesitation I have chosen this one:

Flit flit flit they cry in their bright voices
Showering upon the lawn, the firetail finches
Blowing from nowhere like broken leaves and berries
From some far briar-bush that the wind harries
In a flurry of soft green bodies, red beak and tail;
And flit they do when they have picked what they wanted,
Miles through the mountains again, so small, so undaunted,
As if they can see some sweet and sheltering briar
Formed of their own green flight and tips of fire
Where finches are safe wherever they blow with the gale.

Readers will be relieved to hear that I do not intend to go through the 700-odd species of birds that may be found in Australia. I will not even try to deal with the bowerbirds and the extraordinary mallee fowl whose feat of hatching its eggs in a mound of leaves—keeping the temperature correct to within two degrees—is one of the zoological wonders of the world. I mean to concentrate only on my special favourites. But I cannot leave out all mention of the lyrebird, perhaps the best known—and least seen—bird in Australia, whose display, when the cock raises its lyre-shaped tail over its head, and marvellous powers of song and mimicry have made it famous throughout the world.

When the lyrebird is not displaying it is a quiet, sober, pheasant-like bird which lives in the undergrowth of the coastal ranges. But though shy and secretive it is not as rare as is often supposed. Shortly after I arrived in Australia I was taken to see a lyrebird's nest in French's Forest, just above the busy Roseville Bridge, near Sydney, by Alec Chisholm, one of Australia's most distinguished—and kindest—ornithologists. The nest was just beside a little creek overhung with bushes and we were able to hide quite easily and watch until the hen returned to the nest. She immediately started to clean the nest by removing the chicks' droppings which she then took and dropped into the creek. This ingenious method makes it even more difficult for predators—or ornithologists—to find their nests as the droppings are washed downstream. On another occasion I was boating with my wife and children on the river in Sydney's National Park, just south of the city, when I noticed a lyrebird—a cock this time—feeding on the bank. We allowed the boat to drift in and sat watching it scratching vigorously through the dead leaves a few yards away while other boatloads of picnickers rowed noisily by. The lyrebird hardly looked up.

But alas! I have never seen the cock display. To do that one must know their secret places and go at dawn through the dew-soaked forest to watch them. Is it just laziness that I have never gone or can I steal Judith Wright's excuse?

Over the west side of this mountain,
that's lyrebird country.

I could go down there, they say, in the early morning,
and I'd see them, I'd hear them.

Ten years, and I have never gone.
I'll never go.
I'll never see the lyrebirds—
the few, the shy, the fabulous,
the dying poets.

I should see them, if I lay there in the dew:
first a single movement
like a waterdrop falling, then stillness,
then a brown head, brown eyes,
a splendid bird, bearing
like a crest the symbol of his art,
the high symmetrical shape of the perfect lyre.
I should hear that master practising his art.

No, I have never gone.
Some things ought to be left secret, alone;
some things—birds like walking fables—
ought to inhabit nowhere but the reverence of the heart.

But for me, even before the parrots, come the owls and
birds of prey which have always been my greatest interest.
Here, again, Australia is particularly well-off. Because falcons
and hawks are strong, wide-ranging birds which can fly over
narrow seas, many of them are similar to or even identical
with their fellows in Europe and North America. For instance, the Australian peregrine falcon, brown goshawk, kes-
trel and fork-tailed kite are indistinguishable from these birds
in other countries. But Australia also has many owls and hawks
that are unique. It has two magnificent eagles, the wedge-
tailed eagle, absurdly persecuted in the country where it is
accused—generally wrongly—of taking lambs, and the beautiful white-breasted sea-eagle which is really a large kite and
feeds mainly on dead fish and other offal on the shores. When
I first came to Sydney the sea-eagles were still fairly common
on Pittwater and the estuary of the Hawkesbury. Today they
are rare, though occasionally one can still be seen early in the
morning, flapping heavily over the water or soaring, on wide
wings, on the air currents above the hills. The wedge-tailed
eagle fortunately is still fairly common inland in spite of per-

E

secution. I have stopped the car beside Lake George near Canberra and watched three of these bold, dark, splendid birds—one of the largest eagles in the world—perching together on a tree beside the road. I have several times seen a pair of the much rarer little eagles in the hills near Canberra. The common "whistling eagle" of the plains is not an eagle at all but a large kite, but its easy soaring flight and shrill musical whistle are pleasant things to see and hear.

One of the curiosities of Australian bird-life is that so many birds of prey are very pale or even white, an unlikely colour for a sunburnt country. I have already mentioned the white-breasted sea-eagle whose pale-grey back and snow-white breast and belly make a dazzling picture as it soars over the blue water. Two kites, the letter-winged and black-shouldered species, are also mostly white. I once saw a black-shouldered kite sitting on a gum-tree at the very top of Dead Horse Gap, a high and windy pass in the Snowy Mountains. It looked like a snow-flake in the cold mountain air. Once more—for the last time—I must quote Judith Wright:

> Carved out of strength, the furious kite
> shoulders off the wind's hate.
> The black mark that bars his white
> is the pride and hunger of Cain.
> Perfect, precise, the angry calm
> of his closed body, that snow-storm—
> of his still eye that threatens harm.
> Hunter and force his beauty made
> and turned a bird to a knife-blade.

But the most spectacular of all is the white goshawk. This is an extreme form of a distinct species, the grey goshawk, and is found chiefly in Tasmania and southern Victoria. Alas! I have never seen one outside Taronga Zoo in Sydney, which has a magnificent specimen, though I have seen a grey goshawk in Kuringai Chase. The grey goshawk is beautiful enough—it is a pale, smoky-grey all over—but the white goshawk is spectacular. Snowy-white, with red-gold, fiery eyes, this bold hawk must rival the Greenland and Iceland falcons as the most beautiful of all birds of prey. One of my few surviving ambitions is to see the white goshawk wild and free in the dark forests of Tasmania.

I would like to write about the Australian owls but dare not. My experience of them is too limited. Instead I would strongly recommend to any reader who is interested, a remarkable book by David Fleay called *Nightwatchman of Bush and Plain,* which describes a life-long obsession with, and search for, the rare powerful owl, the masked owl, the sooty owl and other fascinating species. It has photographs of incomparable beauty.

It might be thought that an interest in birds of prey did not fit easily with the life of a busy journalist in Sydney. And of course many species can be seen only in the wild country of the outback and the coastal ranges. Yet it is surprising how many survive in and about the city. I have several times seen peregrine falcons flying over the harbour near the Bridge and it is said that a pair once nested on the Bridge pylon. I have seen a brown hawk—really a falcon—over Chinaman's Beach and a brown goshawk many times at Ball's Head and Berry Island. (One even came and perched on a willow tree outside our house at Lavender Bay.) Kestrels can be seen in many suburbs; I watched a pair swoop on a sparrow in a street in McMahon's Point. (They missed.) Most remarkable of all, a powerful owl—one of our rarest birds—once lived for three years in the suburb of Pymble. For those who do not know Sydney, all these places might fairly be described as being near the heart of the city. Further out it is better still. Where we now live on Pittwater one may see almost anything if one waits long enough. An immature female goshawk spent a day in our garden perched on a lofty spotted gum. Twice we watched her swoop down in a swift, descending curve on some small bird in the scrub below the house. Both times she missed, probably from inexperience. (Not many people realize how difficult it is for a hawk or falcon to catch its prey. A high proportion of attempts end in failure, and it is known that many young birds die each year before they can learn what prey to choose and how to go about it.) It was curious to see this splendid bird, legs wide apart, plunge deep into the foliage of a bush, looking at the same time fiercely proud and slightly foolish while the currawongs and noisy miners stared in astonishment. And one night two boobook owls, one after the other, perched on a tree outside our sitting room and gazed in at us as we sat watching the fading light in the west, before they glided away on soft moth-like wings.

It is moments like these one remembers with delight. Another evening, sitting on the same balcony, we watched thirty black swans—I had time to count them—flying in formation down Pittwater, a thrilling black line drawn across the sunset. A fairy penguin catching a fish in clear shallow water—I could see its beak open and close upon the fish—six feet from where I stood on Paradise Beach while children played and swam all round me. Pelicans soaring in perfect, lazy circles high in the air above Lake George. A peregrine killing and eating a crimson rosella at the foot of the Black Mountain in Canberra. The "insolent emu" stepping delicately over the arid plain on the border of South Australia and New South Wales, with his striped chicks—his not hers, for it is the male emu which looks after the young. A flock of crimson rosellas like bloodstains on the snow of the Brindabella range. Giant wandering albatrosses gliding on infinite white wings over the swell off Avalon. To me, at least, these are not the least of pleasures offered by the Lucky Country. But oh, how I wish that I too were a poet!

R.L.S. IN SYDNEY

I LOVED Robert Louis Stevenson from the moment I read *Kidnapped* and *Treasure Island* as a boy. Fifty years later I still do. I can recognize his faults as a writer: the excessive mannerism of his early style (though not, surely, in the later novels and essays), the slight falsity of his Bohemian pose, the lack of maturity and psychological understanding which mars all but a few of his novels. But I have only to pick up one of his books—say, the delightful *New Arabian Nights* or his description of his first landfall in the South Pacific or, above all, the first three chapters of *Weir of Hermiston*—to surrender immediately to his charm and the subtle cadence of his prose.

But I have also found it easy to identify with Stevenson for quite other reasons. Like him, I was born in "that cold, old huddle of grey hills" which is known as Scotland. Like him I contracted tuberculosis of the lungs when still a young man. Like him I sailed for the South Seas at the age of thirty-eight. Like him I have spent my life divided between a passionate love for my native land and a fierce reaction against the puritanical teaching of the Scottish Kirk. I do not wish to sound conceited. I am aware that the distance between Stevenson and myself as a writer is rather greater than the distance between Sydney and Samoa. Nor, in this age of medical miracles, was tuberculosis for me anything like the fearful disease that ravaged Stevenson throughout his adult life. Yet this common background has given me a special sympathy for Stevenson the man as well as for Stevenson the writer, and for this reason I have found great pleasure in retracing Stevenson's own visits to Sydney.

For it is not commonly known that Stevenson paid four visits to Sydney between 1890 and his death in 1893. Of all the great writers who visited Australia at the end of the nineteenth and beginning of the twentieth centuries—Trollope, Conrad, Kipling, Galsworthy, D. H. Lawrence—Stevenson stayed here longest and, perhaps, liked it best. Indeed there was a brief moment when, according to the closest of his missionary friends, the Reverend W. Clarke, he seriously contemplated settling in Sydney rather than Samoa.

The story, briefly, is this. On 28th June 1888 Robert Louis Stevenson, his American wife Fanny, his stepson Lloyd Osbourne, his stepdaughter Isobel (Belle) Strong, and his mother (always known as "Aunt Maggie"), set sail from San Francisco in the schooner *Casco* which they had chartered for their first voyage to the South Seas. After landing at the Marquesas and Tahiti they reached Honolulu in January 1889 where the schooner was discharged. By then Stevenson had fallen in love with the islands, and his health, which had been so desperate when they set sail from San Francisco that he did not think he would survive the voyage, had greatly improved.

After staying six months in Honolulu, Stevenson and his family set off again in the trading schooner *Equator* in June 1889 to visit the Gilberts and Samoa. This time Stevenson's mother left them to go home to Scotland and his stepdaughter, Belle, was sent to Sydney with her child to await them. Belle's husband, Joe Strong, took her place with the party. They arrived in Samoa in December 1889. Stevenson had then no intention of settling in Samoa and at first did not particularly like the island of Upolu. He still planned to return to England in 1890, travelling by way of Sydney, Ceylon, Suez, and Marseilles after completing a book on the South Seas.

After a few weeks, however, Stevenson began to think of

making his home permanently in Samoa. On a sudden impulse he bought four hundred acres of land near Apia for four thousand dollars, and named it Vailima, which was the Samoan word for "five rivers". Even then it is doubtful whether he and his wife had finally decided to live there or merely to make it an occasional home. Fanny would have liked Honolulu, but Stevenson preferred Samoa because it was "more savage". Having bought the land and left instructions for some of it to be cleared in his absence, he and his family sailed for Sydney in February 1890 in the new Norddeutscher Lloyd steamship *Lubeck* which made a regular passage between Sydney and Samoa. The Stevensons enjoyed the comfort of the *Lubeck* which was to play an important part in their future comings and goings.

The Stevensons arrived in Sydney for the first time on 13th February 1890. Stevenson was not then a world-famous author, but his arrival was noted by the press and welcomed by discerning citizens. Stevenson was made a member of the Union Club, where he stayed during most of his visits; his wife and the rest of the family stayed in lodgings. By 19th February he was writing to Henry James that he was comfortably ensconced "in this excellent, civilized, antipodean, club smoking room". Anyone who remembers the handsome old club in Bligh Street, now replaced by some of the ugliest buildings in Sydney, will understand his pleasure. He quickly began to enjoy himself and wrote to his cousin that "As this is like to be our metropolis, I have tried to lay myself out to be sociable . . . Several niceish people have turned up." One of these was Dr Scot-Skirving, an old friend from his Edinburgh University days, who rang him at the club (Sydney already had the telephone). "Are you the man who acted at the Jenkin's theatricals?" Stevenson asked him. (Jenkin was Professor Fleeming Jenkin of whom R.L.S. wrote a memoire.) He was, and they spent several pleasant evenings together.

Unfortunately there were two contrary omens. The first was the weather, which, as always when Stevenson was in Sydney, was abominable. His arrival seems to have coincided with one of those cyclonic depressions which occasionally afflict us in summer. It was appallingly wet, windy and—by Samoan standards—cold. The second was Fanny. She too noted that the weather was abominable but also remarked on "the cruel stamp very strong on the faces of the passers-by. Louis likes the town, but I don't. I pine for my Isles, ah my Islands." As Stevenson's biographers have noted, when Fanny made up her mind, she generally got her way.

For a time, however, all went well. We have two vivid memories of Stevenson on this first visit. James Tyrrell, then a boy of sixteen working in Angus and Robertson's "old shop" in Castlereagh Street, saw him "walking up the King Street incline dressed in white with a cummerbund and a velvet coat. . . . I have a curiously unreal recollection of his eyes being extraordinarily far apart." The other was a friend of Tighe Ryan's (the editor of *The Antipodean*) who saw him one night at the Union Club in a "mad mood".

> R.L.S., who is the most genial of companions, suddenly rose from his seat and, apparently forgetful of his surroundings, walked hastily up and down. His eyes were ablaze, his gaze intent, fierce and savage. Occasionally he stopped to make a few notes on a slip of paper on the table, then resumed his walk with feverish excitement, his lips moving all the time, as if in conversation with unseen beings. The others smoked silently or read the papers, throwing glances at the spare figure, who seemed to them to have been taken possession of by a foreign devil. He was then engaged on *The Wrecker*, and perhaps it was at this moment, in the club-room, that he inspired the massacre of the crew of the *Flying Scud*.

This is not entirely fanciful. Stevenson was indeed working on *The Wrecker* which he had first planned with Lloyd Osbourne on board the schooner *Equator*. He began writing it in October 1889, and told his publisher that it was "half-done" when he sailed for Sydney in the *Lubeck*. Perhaps one can pinpoint the place he had reached by his reference to the copy of the *Sydney Morning Herald* that Loudon Dodd and Captain Nares found on board the *Flying Scud*. It is doubtful if Stevenson would have thought of this if he had not been reading the paper in the Union Club. But his visit to Sydney was to shape *The Wrecker* in more important ways. It was on a brief trip down the South Coast that he saw the "remittance-man", Norris Carthew, labouring in a railway gang in a flood-washed cutting at South Clifton. It was on a bench in Macquarie Street that he found a shopkeeper's assistant out of a job, "a diminutive, cheerful, red-headed creature" whom he made into Hemstead and to whom he gave a recognizable Australian accent. And it was when wandering through the Domain that he gained those impressions which formed the basis of his famous description:

> Every morning for the next two or three weeks the stroke of ten found Norris, unkempt and haggard, at the lawyer's door. The long day and longer night he spent in the Domain, now on a bench, now on the grass under a norfolk pine, the companion of perhaps the lowest class on earth, the Larrikins of Sydney. Morning after morning, the dawn behind the lighthouse recalled him from slumber; and he would stand and gaze upon the changing east, the fading lenses, the smokeless city, and the many-armed and many masted harbour growing slowly clear under his eyes. His bed-fellows (so to call them) were less active; they lay sprawled upon the grass and benches, the dingy men, the frowsty women, prolonging their late repose; and Carthew wandered among the sleeping bodies alone, and cursed the incurable stupidity of their behaviour. Day brought a new society of nursery-maids and children, and fresh-dressed and (I am sorry to say) tight-laced maidens, and gay people in rich traps; upon the skirts of which Carthew and "the other blackguards"—his own bitter phrase—skulked, and chewed grass, and looked on. Day passed, the light died, the green and leafy precinct sparkled with lamps or lay in shadow, and the round of the night began again—the loitering women, the lurking men, the sudden outburst of screams, the sound of flying feet. "You mayn't believe it," says Carthew, "but I got to that pitch that I didn't care a hang. I have been wakened out of my sleep to hear a woman screaming, and I have only turned upon the other side. Yes, it's a queer place, where the dowagers and the kids walk all day, and at night you can hear people bawling for help as if it was the Forest of Bondy, with the lights of a great town all round, and parties spinning through in cabs from Government House and dinner with my lord!"

The Wrecker is not one of Stevenson's best books, though it is not as bad as some critics have said. And it must always have a special interest for Sydney and San Francisco because these cities play so large a part in it.

The other literary event that marked Stevenson's first

visit to Sydney was his famous "Open Letter to Dr Hyde". I cannot help thinking that too much fuss has been made about this letter largely because it was written in Sydney, but for what they are worth the facts are these. Shortly after his arrival Stevenson happened to read, in the *Presbyterian* of 26th October 1889, a letter about Father Damien by an American missionary, the Reverend C. M. Hyde of Honolulu. Father Damien was the famous Belgian missionary who had died in April 1889 of leprosy contracted while nursing the sick in the leper settlement on the island of Molokai in Hawaii. In this letter Dr Hyde said that Damien was "a coarse, dirty man, headstrong and bigoted. He was not sent to Molokai, but went there without orders. . . . He was not a pure man in his relations with women, and the leprosy of which he died should be attributed to his vices and carelessness. Others have done much for the lepers, our own ministers, the government physicians and so forth, but never with the Catholic idea of meriting eternal life."

In fact this was a personal letter, which, however unjust, was never intended for publication. Stevenson did not know this and all his most generous instincts were aroused. He had himself visited the leper settlement at Molokai in 1889, shortly after Damien's death, and had been greatly moved by what he saw. He had talked to the sisters and others on the island about Father Damien and had formed a passionate admiration for his work. Stevenson had no illusions about Damien. He himself had written to Colvin, his friend and editor, of Damien's "weaknesses and worse. . . . It was a European peasant: dirty, bigoted, untruthful, unwise, tricky but superb with generosity, residual candour and fundamental good humour . . . a man with all the grime and paltriness of mankind, but a saint and a hero all the more for that." He now determined that he must answer Dr Hyde at once.

Stevenson wrote the "Letter to Dr Hyde" in the Union Club on 25th February 1890.* Earlier Dr Scot-Skirving met him

* I have often wondered how Stevenson came to read Dr Hyde's letter, which had appeared in very small type in the *Presbyterian* nearly six months earlier. By chance I think I may have stumbled on the answer. Cardinal Moran, then Catholic Archbishop of Sydney, had attacked Dr Hyde's letter in a sermon preached at Saint Mary's Cathedral on Sunday, 24th February. I

in the street and asked him what he was doing with himself. "Well," Stevenson replied, "I propose to devote myself to writing a libel, but it will be a justified and righteous one." It was. I do not propose to quote it here, but the "Letter to Dr Hyde" is one of the noblest pieces of invective ever penned. Every line is quivering with passionate indignation. But it is clearly libellous. It is said—on rather meagre evidence—that Stevenson first offered the letter to the editor of the *Sydney Morning Herald*, William Curnow, who refused to publish it. If it is true, I cannot blame him. I would probably have done the same. He then offered it to the editor of the *Australian Star*, J. M. Sanders, who was also more cautious than his own account suggests. The *Australian Star* did eventually publish the letter on 24th May—but not until it had first appeared in the *Scots Observer* in Edinburgh on 3rd and 10th May and in the Honolulu *Elele* on 10th May. Stevenson had then left Sydney. Dr Hyde never brought an action and the matter was closed. The "letter" was also published in Sydney as a pamphlet with a limited edition of twenty-five copies. This is a much valued collector's item to those who care about these things. The Mitchell Library has two copies.

Shortly after writing the "Letter to Dr Hyde", Stevenson fell ill. Whether it was really the wet and windy weather or merely the normal risk of cold and 'flu to which he was again exposed after his long isolation in the South Pacific one cannot be sure. But the illness was serious enough and brought on the first haemorrhage he had had since leaving Honolulu. By 7th March he was writing to his friend Charles Baxter: "This visit to Sydney has smashed me handsomely; and yet I made myself a prisoner here in the club upon first arrival. This is not encouraging for future visitations; Sydney winter —or, I might almost say, Sydney spring, for I came when the worst was over—is so small an affair compared to our June depressions at home in Scotland." (From this letter one must reach the extraordinary conclusion that R.L.S. then believed that March was the end of Sydney's winter instead of Sydney's summer. Later he got it right. Writing to Charles Baxter

---

have little doubt that it was this sermon, reported in the Sydney press on Monday, 25th February, which inspired Stevenson to look up the letter and write his famous reply.

from Noumea in August the same year he explained that he is staying there "partly to shorten my stay in the extreme cold —hear me with my extreme! moi qui suis originaire d'Edinbourg—of Sydney at this season".)

Stevenson was well looked after in the Union Club. He had a fire in his bedroom and his only complaint was that he was not allowed to play his flageolet for fear of disturbing the other members. But he did not get better and by the end of March Fanny was seriously worried. She made up her mind that she must get him away to the South Seas again if he was to live, and started desperately to look for a suitable ship. Eventually she found the *Janet Nicoll*, a 600-ton trading schooner (part sail, part steam) with a mixed Melanesian and Polynesian crew, which was shortly leaving Sydney for a cruise to New Zealand and Micronesia. At first the owners, Henderson and Macfarlane, refused to take passengers, especially a woman and a sick man, but finally gave in to Fanny's pleading. On 10th April Stevenson, "rolled like a mummy in a blanket", was carried to the wharf and rowed to the steamer —there was, of course, a dock strike at the time!—and on 11th April they sailed. Once again Lloyd Osbourne went with them.

The *Janet Nicoll* was called the "Jumping Jenny" because she rolled so abominably in bad weather. She was far from comfortable and stank of copra, but Stevenson loved her. He loved the sea, the sailors, and even in this case his fellow-passengers, Harry Henderson, the owner, Ben Hird, the supercargo, and Jack Buckland or "Tin Jack", the engaging young scamp of a trader who became a close friend of Stevenson and formed the model for Tommy Hadden in *The Wrecker* as well as providing material for parts of *The Ebb-tide* and *The Beach of Falesa*. Stevenson always had a weakness for rogues and vagabonds—which is one reason why he liked Sydney. He dedicated *Island Nights' Entertainment* to these "Three Old Shipmates".

Stevenson was still ill when they reached New Zealand but recovered quickly when they headed north again for warmer seas. Their only real adventure was when, one day out from New Zealand, Jack Buckland's fireworks, which he was taking to the islands to impress the natives, exploded in the cabin, setting fire to a trunk containing Stevenson's manuscripts. Only quick action by Fanny prevented the crew from throwing it overboard.

The *Janet Nicoll* finally reached Samoa in July but only stayed long enough for Stevenson and Fanny to inspect their property and give instructions for a temporary "cottage" to be built for them. It then sailed on to Noumea where Stevenson got off, leaving his family to sail back to Sydney alone. He wished partly to see the New Hebrides and partly, as noted, to avoid staying too long in Sydney in the cold weather. His health was now much better. He then took another ship sailing to Sydney and rejoined his family there in August. This was his second visit.

Once again he stayed at the Union Club and Fanny in lodgings, though later he joined her at the Oxford Hotel in King Street. (There is a story, based on dubious evidence, that when the Stevenson's arrived, wearing the clothing of the islands and loaded with Polynesian curios, the "best hotel in Sydney" refused to take them in. Later the manager discovered his mistake and tried to get them back, but they remained at the Oxford.) And once again Stevenson promptly caught a cold. This event was decisive. It made Stevenson realize not merely that he could not stay in Sydney but that he could never return to England. That month he wrote to Henry James from the Union Club:

> I must tell you plain—I can't tell Colvin—I do not think that I shall come to England more than once, and then it'll be to die. Health I enjoy in the tropics; even here, which they call sub- or semi-tropical, I come only to catch cold. I have not been out since my arrival; live here in a nice bed-room by the fireside, and read books and letters from Henry James, and send out to get his "Tragic Muse", only to be told they can't be had as yet in Sydney, and have altogether a placid time. But I can't go out! The thermometer was down to 50 the other day—no temperature for me, Mr. James; how should I do in England? I fear not at all.

From that moment Stevenson and his wife decided to live permanently in Samoa. He got a Sydney architect to prepare him a plan for a large house at Vailima, though the plan had later to be abandoned since it would have cost twenty-thousand dollars to build! His stepson Lloyd Osbourne was sent home to England to sell their house, "Skerryvore", at Bournemouth and bring out the furniture. His mother was invited to join them. They themselves booked their passage on the *Lubeck* which was due to sail from Sydney on 4th September. In the meantime, in spite of his illness, he made some new acquaintances, including Bertram Wise, the brilliant constitutional lawyer and politician, who became his best friend in Sydney; Professor Anderson Stuart, a fellow Scot, who founded the Medical School at Sydney University; and Julian Ashton, the painter, who had met him briefly on his first visit. In his *Now Came Still Evening On* Julian Ashton recalls:

> I saw Stevenson again on his second visit when he spent a good deal of his time in bed, his strength having been sapped by a long attack of his pulmonary trouble. I often went to see him and usually found him hard at work writing lying down. His hours of work were from eight to twelve, after which, if he felt well enough, he went abroad.
>
> On another occasion he pointed to his waste-paper basket, "Look at that, Ashton. There's stuff there that my publisher would give golden guineas for." I asked him why it was in the basket, and he answered, "Because it doesn't help my story."

It was on this second visit to Sydney, too, that Stevenson "discovered" Kipling. Rudyard Kipling's first books had just arrived in Sydney in a paperback edition—he himself had passed through Sydney the year before, in 1889—and Stevenson sent out for them. They were probably *Plain Tales from the Hills, Departmental Ditties* and *Letters of Marque*. Stevenson was deeply impressed. He left orders with a Sydney bookshop to send everything Kipling wrote to him in Samoa and wrote in generous terms to Henry James:

> Kipling is by far the most promising young man who has appeared since—ahem—I appeared. He amazes me by his precocity and various endowment. . . . Well, we begin to be old fogies now; and it was high time *something* rose to take our places. Certainly Kipling has the gifts; the fairy god-mothers were all tipsy at his christening: what will he do with them?

Stevenson and Fanny sailed for their new "home" in the *Lubeck* on 4th September 1890. Two missionaries, the Reverend Dr George Brown and the Reverend J. Chalmers, sailed with them as far as Tonga and both later recalled their pleasure at Stevenson's marvellous gift for story-telling in the smoking-room. Both men became his friends. They reached Samoa in October, and Stevenson and Fanny moved into their little three-room hut or "cottage" on Vailima and began to prepare their plans for a bigger house. Although they had made up their minds to stay in Samoa, Sydney always remained in a sense their "metropolis" and shopping centre. Stevenson had his boots made by Chorley and his suits by Alley. They had an agent there who supplied them with goods they could not buy in Samoa and sent Fanny plants and trees for her garden. They got regular mail from Britain and the United States either on the *Lubeck* from Sydney or on the *Mariposa* from San Francisco. Members of the family thought nothing of hopping onto the *Lubeck* for a quick trip to Sydney, and Stevenson himself was to visit the city twice more before he died.

Indeed it was only three months later, in January 1891, that Stevenson returned on the *Lubeck* for his third visit. This time he went alone because Fanny was ill with earache. His purpose was to meet his mother, who had arrived in Sydney from Scotland in December and was going to join them in Samoa. One cannot help thinking that Fanny's reluctance to go on this occasion may have been influenced by this. These two strong-minded women, mother and daughter-in-law, did not always see eye to eye. It was an unlucky voyage, as the *Lubeck* broke a shaft in her engine-room, but in spite of this she limped into Sydney on 19th January, only a few days late. Stevenson joined his mother at the Oxford Hotel where Mrs Stevenson found her "dear boy looking brown and well". In spite of this he promptly fell ill again with what he later described as "a smoking hot little malady", "a swingeing sharp attack". Sydney was plainly disastrous. He was able to take his mother once to hear the speeches in the Domain on a Sunday—Mrs Stevenson wrote that "at least they were not monotonous"—and James Tyrrell remembered them visiting Angus and Robertson's bookshop together, but for the most part he lay ill in bed. His mother nursed him devotedly—like most mothers she probably enjoyed it!—and they sailed again on the *Lubeck* on 19th February with Stevenson still very ill. During the voyage to Samoa he wrote to Sidney Colvin:

> It is vastly annoying that I can't even go to Sydney without an attack, and heaven knows my life was anodyne. I only once dined with anybody; at the club with Wise; worked all morning—a terrible dead pull; a month only produced the imperfect embryos of two chapters; lunch at the boarding-house, played on my pipe; went out and did some of my messages; dined at a French restaurant, and returned to play draughts, whist and Van John with my family. This makes a cheery life after Samoa; but it isn't what you call burning the candle at both ends, is it?

The next two years, from February 1891 to January 1893, were the happiest of Stevenson's life. His health recovered to a point where he could ride and swim and take his share of the work in clearing and planting at Vailima. The big house they had planned was eventually built and then extended, and Stevenson gathered round him his family and Samoan servants who together formed his "clan". (Like Scott before him at Abbotsford, Stevenson liked to play the laird at Vailima.) His fame was now established and he was earning large sums from royalties, though both he and Fanny were recklessly extravagant. Moreover this was a period of great creative energy. He finished off *The Wrecker*, collaborated with his stepson, Lloyd Osbourne, in the much more powerful and effective "thriller", *The Ebb-tide*, wrote that little masterpiece *The Beach of Falesa*, based on his own experiences cruising in the South Seas, and began *Weir of Hermiston*.

There were, of course, troubles in paradise (there always are!). Isobel's husband, Joe Strong, proved to be an irresponsible drunk and idler who had affairs with the Samoan maids and had to be sent away. Later they were divorced, but for the rest of Stevenson's life Belle devoted herself to her stepfather and took down in longhand all his books from dictation. Stevenson's mother was at first appalled by the discomforts and primitive conditions of life in Samoa and hinted more than once that it might be more convenient to live "in the colonies"—by which she meant New South Wales. For a time, indeed, she went back to Sydney until the big house was ready.

Stevenson and Fanny became deeply involved in the complicated politics of Samoa, bedevilled by the iniquitous agreement between the United States, Britain and Germany at Berlin in 1889 which placed the islands under tripartitite control. They warmly championed their friend Chief Mataafa both against the Germans, who deposed him, and against his rival, Chief Laupepa Malietoa. (As if intertribal and international politics were not bad enough, this quarrel had religious undertones. Mataafa was a devout Catholic convert; Malietoa was a nominal Protestant.) At one time both the German and British High Commissioners threatened to have the Stevensons deported.

It was the troubled situation in Samoa that provided one of Stevenson's two rather curious links with Sydney during these two years. The Governor of New South Wales was then Victor Albert George Child-Villiers, the seventh Earl of Jersey. In August 1892 his wife, the Countess of Jersey, visited Samoa with her brother, Captain Leigh, and her daughter, Lady Margaret Villiers. The party met Stevenson (as all visitors to the island did) and Stevenson roused Lady Jersey's interest in Samoan affairs and even persuaded her to go with him to see Mataafa, who had been deposed by the Germans and removed from his home. Since this was clearly very indiscreet for the wife of the Governor of New South Wales, Lady Jersey, a bold and independent woman, pretended to be Stevenson's cousin, "Amelia Balfour". Naturally this trick did not deceive anyone, and the incident led to a stern reprimand from the British Government and, very nearly, to a diplomatic incident. On her return to Sydney, however, Lady Jersey published, of course anonymously, a curious pamphlet on Samoa called *An Object of Pity, or the Man Haggard, A Romance by Many Competent Hands* to which Stevenson contributed a dedication and one chapter, entitled "Late, ever Late". ("The Man Haggard" was Mr Bazett Michael Haggard, the British Land Commissioner in Samoa and brother of Rider Haggard, the author.) Elaborate attempts were made to conceal the authorship and even the origin of

F

this pamphlet, which carried the imprint of Amsterdam. Only sixty-eight copies were printed. It is now extremely rare.

It may be noted that Fanny, a staunch American democrat, did not like the Countess of Jersey. She noted acidly in her journal that the aristocratic visitors were "a selfish champagne Charley set, with the exception of the daughter, Lady Margaret . . . Lady Jersey tall and leggy and awkward, with bold black eyes and sensual mouth; very selfish and greedy of admiration, a touch of vulgarity, courageous as a man and reckless as a woman."

The other link with Sydney in those years was the famous Nerli portrait. "Count" Nerli was an Italian artist who apparently had a claim to the title of Marchese in his native land. He migrated to Melbourne in 1886 and later moved to Sydney. In 1892 he went to Samoa with the idea of doing some sketches of island life, and while there someone suggested that he should do a portait of Stevenson. Stevenson agreed and was so pleased with the result that he wrote the well-known verses:

> Did ever mortal man hear tell of sae singular a ferlie,
> As the coming to Apia here of the painter, Mr. Nerli?
> He came and O! for a hunner pound, of a' he was the perli.
> He took a thraw to paint mysel', he painted late and early;
> O wow! the many a yawn I've yawned in the beard of Mr. Nerli!
> Whiles I would sleep an' whiles would wake, and whiles was mair than surly,
> I wondered sair, as I sat there, forninst the eyes of Nerli
> Or will he paint me the way I want, as bonnie as a girlie,
> Or will he paint me as an ugly tyke, and be damned to Mr. Nerli!
> But still and on and whichever it is, he is a canty Kerli;
> The Lord protect the back and neck of honest Mr. Nerli.

The subsequent history of this portrait is both complicated and obscure. James Tyrrell says that Nerlie eventually sold it to Angus and Robertson, whose "new shop" in Castlereagh Street he was then managing, for twenty-five pounds. Later Tyrrell sold it to Professor Anderson Stuart for forty-five pounds. The professor took it to Edinburgh and offered it to the Scottish National Gallery only to find that they already had a duplicate! Professor Stuart took his own copy back to

Australia where it changed hands several times before being sold to an American collector for five hundred pounds. In fact there is a suspicion that Count Nerli, that canny man, did *three* versions of the portrait, one of which he disposed of in New Zealand. Poor fellow, he badly needed the money. Tyrrell tells a story of G. V. F. Mann, a former director of the Art Gallery of New South Wales, colliding with Nerli who was rushing downstairs from his studio with a parcel under his arm. "It's all right, Mann," cried Nerli, "I have saved 'Robert Louis'!" It turned out that the bailiffs were upstairs.

The idyll of these last two years came to an end in January 1893, when an epidemic of influenza devastated Samoa. It was hardly to be expected that when so many of the natives were suffering—they were fearfully prone to this disease—the Stevenson family would escape. First Stevenson's mother, then Fanny, then other members of the family and finally Stevenson himself went down with an attack. Ominously this brought on a haemorrhage—"my old friend Bluidy Jack"— the first he had had for a long time. It was during this illness, when Stevenson was confined to bed and not allowed to speak, that he attempted to continue the dictation of *Weir of Hermiston* to Belle in deaf and dumb sign language—an astonishing example of Stevenson's determination. He rarely complained, but in September 1893, shortly before his death, he wrote to George Meredith:

> For fourteen years I have not had one day's real health; I have wakened sick and gone to bed weary; and I have done my work unflinchingly. I have written in bed, and written out of it, written in haemorrhages, written in sickness, written torn by coughing, written when my head swam for weakness; and for so long, it seems to me I have won my wager and recovered my glove. . . .

Stevenson's mother was sent to Sydney alone to recuperate, but Stevenson recovered only to have a relapse in February. The family then decided that they all needed a holiday and decided to go for another trip to Sydney. This time they sailed on the *Mariposa*, not the *Lubeck*. Fanny and Belle went with Stevenson, but Lloyd Osbourne stayed in Samoa to look after the property.

This, the fourth and last visit to Sydney, was quite different from all the others. To begin with, Stevenson was now a world-famous author. When he first came to Sydney in 1890 he had a small but distinguished reputation as the author of *Treasure Island, Kidnapped* and *Dr Jekyll and Mr Hyde*. *The Master of Ballantrae* had been published in 1889 but had probably not reached Sydney. Since then his fame had grown rapidly. The very popular *The Wrecker* had been published in 1892 and *The Beach of Falesa* had appeared in serial form the same year, though it and the two other South Seas stories, *The Bottle Imp* and *The Isle of Voices*, were not published in book form as *Island Nights' Entertainments* until April 1893. Stevenson had also become famous by his dispatches to *The Times* championing the Samoan people against the Great Powers.

Secondly, in spite of his recent attack, Stevenson was a much stronger man. He was able and determined to savour "the sweet smell of success" for the first time in his life. This time it was Fanny, rather than Stevenson, who was ill—she was suffering from gallstones and often in great pain—and Stevenson was left to go round by himself or with Belle. Although there is no doubt of Stevenson's genuine love and devotion to his wife, it often seemed that he could enjoy himself more with his young stepson and stepdaughter than with Fanny who was, after all, ten years older than he was.

Because Stevenson did more on this visit we know more. Indeed we can trace his activities in considerable detail. Unfortunately not all the evidence is reliable. Some of those who met him confused his different visits in their memories. Others naturally tended to exaggerate the number of times they had dined with him or met him. Indeed, since he was only in Sydney three weeks, from 28th February 1893 to 20th March, and was certainly ill for some of that time, it is almost impossible to see how he fitted in all the engagements he is alleged to have kept!

The *Mariposa* arrived in Sydney on 28th February. Stevenson was met by the press and immediately gave an interview to the reporter of the *Sydney Morning Herald*, the first of several he granted during this visit in spite of his normal dislike of the press. Most of this interview was concerned with events in Samoa, which were then of considerable interest to Australians, but the reporter was able to assure his readers that the report of Stevenson's death which had reached Sydney from America was much exaggerated and that his "physique is vastly improved since his last visit. . . . Today he is well set-up, has the glow of health in his countenance, and altogether bears testimony to the beneficent effects of the Samoan climate." In reporting his views on Samoa the reporter added cautiously that "he is apt to express his views in language rather too plain for publication in Australia"!

But if one really wants to discover Stevenson's thoughts and movements during his last stay in Sydney, one must go to the *Presbyterian and Australian Witness*, then a remarkably well-written and well-produced weekly which, I am glad to say, still exists. The plain truth is that the *Presbyterian* scooped the rest of the Sydney press hollow. Between its issues of 4th March and 1st April 1893, it published three long interviews with Stevenson, all corrected by his own hand, and published the longest versions (also approved by the master) of two of his three addresses. Since at least two of the interviews are still of great interest, this was not a bad achievement for a church paper.

Stevenson was a reporter's dream. He expressed strong and interesting views in clear and vigorous language. The first interview, which appeared on 4th March 1893, was almost entirely on Samoan politics and is of lesser interest today, thought it gave the reporter an opportunity to introduce Stevenson which he seized with both hands:

> The personality of a famous writer is always interesting to his readers—and who is not a reader of Stevenson's enthralling books? Mr Stevenson may still be called a young man. He is tall and thin, and walks with a slight stoop of the shoulders. His face is refined and beautiful. Looking on it one would at once say, "This is a man of intellect". But looking into the full, glowing, dark eyes, one would go further and say, "This is a man of genius".

The issue of 18th March had the text of a paper Stevenson had written to the Women's Missionary Association on Missions in the South Seas for his mother, who had joined the family in Sydney, to read for him. (The meeting was held at Quong Tart's rooms, which in the circumstances seems a very suitable rendezvous!) In this paper Stevenson admitted that he had conceived a great prejudice against missions before he went to the South Seas; since living there "that prejudice was first reduced and then annihilated". But he went on to give the missionaries what we would now regard as excellent advice—not to try to destroy the islanders' culture and traditions but to accept them and build on them.

On 25th March the *Presbyterian* published a second long "interview"—in reality an article—in which Stevenson denounced the Labour Traffic which was still providing black labour from the islands to work on the sugar fields of Queensland. This strong, vigorous and enlightened statement was surely of the greatest interest to Australians, and it is extraordinary that it was almost entirely ignored at the time—the *Presbyterian* put this down to the jealousy of the Sydney press which had been scooped by a "church paper"—and seems to have been totally overlooked ever since. Indeed I had never seen a reference to it until I read it for myself. Some of it is still worth quoting.

Stevenson began by questioning whether the Queensland Government's attempts to supervise this evil traffic could possibly be effective. In 1870 that Government had passed an Act requiring blackbirders (or "recruiters" as they were politely called) to carry a government agent to ensure that islanders came willingly. But, as Stevenson quite correctly pointed out, "a ship arrives with a Government Agent on board. In the Western Pacific Islands it is impossible that he should know one language out of eighty. How can he tell whether these people came of free will or under club and cooking-oven? He never can. As a matter of fact, if these people have consented at all, they have consented in the single endeavour to save their lives."

Stevenson conceded that there were cases where the recruiter might even appear as a boon to the islanders. Suppression of infanticide by the missionaries—the islanders' only method of birth-control—had caused overpopulation in some of the islands. A bad season might cause such famine that to volunteer as labour might be the only alternative to starvation. "In the Western Islands those who go as labour would in any case be eaten if they stayed at home. I don't know if life is worth living, as people say nowadays. But if the chance were offered me between what is called volunteering and being made collops of, I should have a try at the volunteering. When the Duke of Atholl raised his volunteers, a man saw a cart passing on the road and filled with men in shackles. He asked who these were and was informed they were the Atholl volunteers. . . . And yet—and yet—there has probably never been anywhere in the world anything more hideous than the Labour traffic. I have been intimate with dozens of blackbirders. I have heard their stories, and I am merciful to your readers in not repeating them." Stevenson said he was certain that kidnapping still continued in spite of all denials. "I believe, in fact, that today, and possibly as we sit here talking, unvizored kidnapping is being practised in the Islands."

It is interesting—and further evidence of Stevenson's interest and knowledge of the subject—that he paid a deserved tribute to Sir Samuel Griffith, the Premier of Queensland, who had tried to stop the evil traffic. Sir Samuel, he said, had been the "sole guarantee" against abuse and now that guarantee had gone. Stevenson ended his interview with a general statement which must have seemed startling and even shocking to many white men at that time but which has proved all too true: "On the whole, the influence of whites in the islands strikes me as far from beneficial, and the more whites, the worse is the effect. A single trader, even the most atrocious scoundrel, is rapidly conquered by his medium, adopts Island civility and decorum, even if he had none of his own when he came there. But as soon as the whites are in a considerable body, the work of de-civilization proceeds merrily. I said 'de-civilization', but, if you insist on it, I will say 'debarbarization'. At least it is a process towards the worse." Is it not astonishing that so noble and prescient a statement, by a world-famous author, should have been so totally forgotten?

The *Presbyterian's* last interview, which did not appear until 1st April, after Stevenson had left Sydney, is better known and has been reprinted. After getting in a few digs at his old enemies Cederkranz and Pilsach in Samoa—how R.L.S. must have enjoyed those names!—Stevenson was at last

persuaded to talk about literature. He smiled when the inter-
viewer compared his mastery of English to Ruskin's. "Read
Arrows of the Chace, and see if I can write as well as he," was
his reply.

> He went on to say that he had deliberately tried to form a
> good style. He wrote *The Wrecker* in collaboration with Mr
> Osbourne. They talked over the plot and the characters and
> Mr Osbourne wrote the first copy of the book. Then he himself
> worked it all over, rewriting every line. In answer to a straight
> question, Mr Stevenson said that his favourite among his books
> was *Kidnapped.* Mrs Stevenson, who had just entered the room,
> said that she liked best his *Life of Fleeming Jenkin.* "I cried
> over that book and never over anything else of his", she added.
> Mr Stevenson said that he believed, as a piece of literature,
> *Thrawn Janet* was the best piece of work he had done.

That interview probably took place in the old Oxford
Hotel, which was one of several places where Stevenson's
family stayed on this visit.

Stevenson himself spent some time at the Union Club,
but the Stevensons also took lodgings for a time first in Macquarie Street and then in Richmond Terrace, which no
longer exists, near the Domain. One suspects it was there that
Tighe Ryan, editor of the *Catholic Press* and *The Antipodean,* found him

> snugly ensconced in an easy-chair, one leg on the other, a book
> on his knee, and a smoking cigarette in his right hand which
> hung loosely over the arm of the chair. A glass of sherry was
> within reach on a little round table, occupying the only space
> not filled by books, magazines, women's hats, and photographs
> —the books being mostly presentation copies of poems which
> poured in upon him the moment it was announced that the
> master was in Sydney. Wreaths of light-blue smoke were float-
> ing about the room. He had just risen from an afternoon nap
> and sleep, he said, was still in his head. I carried away in my
> mind that evening recollections of much that was characteristic
> of the novelist—the tones of the low, clear but soft voice, with
> the slight Scotch accent which added to the picturesqueness of
> the phrases; the rare gesture; the thin, bronzed face, changing
> with every mood; the fine sparkling eyes so far apart; the active

figure, so sparse that in a wind storm it might require the leaden shoes of Philetas.

I do not altogether trust Tighe Ryan's other reminiscences, which suggest an almost hectic activity by R.L.S.—"the evenings in the Old French Club, or at the Australian or Athenaeum Clubs, which became mornings before Stevenson's gaiety and brilliant talk allowed the company to leave". One likes to think, however, that there were at least some of these enchanted evenings.

Stevenson was naturally bombarded with invitations to lecture or speak at lunches and dinners. He certainly accepted two of these; he may have accepted more. (Much later, when he was thinking idly of a lecture tour to the United States, strongly opposed by Fanny, he said: "You remember the good time I had in Sydney, speaking to all the clubs and societies. I'd have walked ten miles to speak to an infants' school!") The two he certainly accepted were an invitation to address the General Assembly of the Presbyterian Church of New South Wales at a luncheon, and an invitation to speak at a lunch in his honour by the Cosmopolitan Club, a club of Bohemians, many of them European expatriates.

The General Assembly of the Presbyterian Church met at Saint Stephen's Church, Phillip Street, on 7th March. On 9th March the *Herald* announced that Stevenson was expected to address the Assembly at a luncheon at the Australia Hotel that day, but at the last moment he was forced to send a letter of apology that, "owing to the disastrous change in the weather, he was compelled to seek safety in that inglorious spot, my bed". (Once again Stevenson had appallingly bad luck with the weather. His arrival in Sydney coincided with heavy rain and floods in Queensland and the North Coast.) However, he was well enough to be the Assembly's guest at lunch at the Australia Hotel on 14th March when he made a delightful and witty speech. He chose as his text "Is Saul also among the prophets?" but decided that he had a very good right to be there. "In the first place I am a Scotsman—but upon that I will not dwell. In the second place, I am an old and, I hope I may be allowed to say, a very good Presbyterian, the proof of which, I may say, is that I have sat out a sermon of an hour and thirty minutes. . . . In the third place, I am a grandson of the manse and a great-grandson of the manse...."

Two days later he was the guest of the Cosmopolitan Club with Mr Kowalski in the chair. This time he skilfully altered his matter to suit his very different audience. He spoke of his lonely life in Samoa and said how much he missed convivial gaiety of that kind. Then he went on to speak of France, the "Mother of the Arts", his second country, and of his dream to visit Paris once again, "to walk through the Louvre, to gaze on the Seine, and, if you will excuse a terrible anti-climax, to enter a French restaurant, drink good wine, and meet French gentlemen!" One of the guests, F. M. Bladen, then the Public Librarian, said later, "I never saw a man who looked so ill or spoke so well"—a good phrase, but did he really look so ill on this visit? Others did not think so and photographs taken then do not suggest it.

There is no doubt that Stevenson enjoyed these occasions. They appealed to his nature, which, as David Daiches says, was always torn between the Presbyterian moralist and the romantic Bohemian. On his way home in the *Mariposa* he wrote to Sidney Colvin about this: "As for me I was entertained at the General Assembly of the Presbyterian Church, lunched at a sort of artistic club; made speeches at both, and may therefore be said to have been, like Saint Paul, all things to all men. . . . Take it for all in all, it was huge fun."

But these formal appearances were by no means Stevenson's only activities on this last visit. He visited the University and signed the visitors' book, was the guest of the Royal Exchange and was invited to Government House, where his old acquaintances, Lord and Lady Jersey, were on the point of retiring. (Stevenson is alleged to have said that he would go only if he could wear his white suit and red cummerbund.) Archibald, the famous editor of the *Bulletin*, took him one day to see the artists' colony at Balmoral, where he met his old friend Julian Ashton, Arthur Streeton, Tom Roberts, A. J. Daplyn, B. E. Minns, and other well-known painters. Percy Spence did a pencil sketch of him there which is now in the National Portrait Gallery, London. Characteristically, however, Stevenson seems to have most enjoyed talking to the cook, "Old Ben", an old sea-dog with a store of improbable tales.

There was also shopping. Since Fanny was ill, Stevenson and Belle enjoyed going round the shops together. They bought a dress suit for Stevenson, dresses for Fanny and Belle, topaz rings engraved with their initials. Stevenson had his photograph taken several times—he was exceedingly vain about his appearance!—both by himself and with his family. Two portraits taken of him at this time are reproduced in J. A. Hammerton's *Stevensoniana*: they are both excellent but are not attributed by Hammerton to any particular photographer. One may have been taken by Falk and the other by Kerry. On their way back from one of these fashionable photographers Stevenson took Belle for fun into a cheap photographers where they had to stand in a queue and put their heads through a frame. It cost sixpence. No record exists of this, but in 1949 Mr Val Waller, who was working for Freeman's Studio in George Street, found a copy of a very fine photograph of Stevenson, Fanny, Belle and his mother— all looking very handsome and distinguished indeed—in the studio's files. It was dated 1891, but this must be an error since neither Belle nor Fanny was in Sydney with Stevenson during his third visit in 1891. Indeed the only time all four were in Sydney together was during this fourth visit in 1893. Somewhat hesitatingly, therefore, I attribute this photograph to 1893 though it seems a trifle excessive to have your photograph taken four times by different photographers in one visit! Moreover he also found time to sit for a portrait by a French sculptor (unknown) who gave the finished work to Stevenson. Later he wrote to St Gaudens, the American sculptor who had done the famous medallion of Stevenson in 1889, and told him: "I mustn't criticise a present, and he had very little time to do it. It is thought by my family to be an excellent likeness of Mark Twain."

Stevenson thoroughly enjoyed his first and only taste of fame. As he wrote to Sidney Colvin, "I found my fame much grown on this return to civilization. Digito monstrari is a new experience; people all looked at me in the streets in Sydney; and it was very queer." J. W. Ellison, one of the few writers who have even mentioned Stevenson's visits to Sydney, says that "when he marched into the dining room of the Victoria, the leading Sydney hotel, looking distinguished in his especially tailored evening clothes, with Fanny by his side in a handsome black velvet evening gown, all the patrons turned to look, and the waiters murmured 'Stevenson!' " If this happened, and I dare say it did, it can only have happened once. In the diary he kept on the *Mariposa* afterwards Stevenson noted that "poor Fanny had very little fun on her visit, having been most of the time on a diet of maltine and slops—and this while the rest of us were rioting on oysters and mushrooms. . . . Take it for all in all, it was huge fun and even Fanny had some lively sport at the beginning; Belle and I all through. We got Fanny a dress on the sly, gaudy black velvet and Duchesse lace. And alas; she was only able to wear it once. But we hope to see more of it at Samoa; it really is lovely. . . ."

On the other hand I find it hard to believe Ellison's story that Stevenson found a "bellboy" so absorbed in reading *Treasure Island* that he could not be roused. It sounds the kind of tale that is always told of famous authors. Another story told by James Tyrrell I find equally incredible. A cleaner in Augus and Robertson's shop, whom Henry Lawson always called "The Duchess", also did some charring for the Stevenson party. R.L.S. is alleged to have thought so well of her that he offered her a housekeeper's job in Samoa. However, The Duchess, a confirmed Sydneyite, turned the offer down. When Tyrrell asked her what she remembered most about Stevenson, she replied: "Louis could spit farther than any man I ever knew." It is an amusing story, but I do not believe that Stevenson would have offered her a job in Samoa where he had a household of native servants, or that she would call him "Louis" in 1893, or that Stevenson, a refined and sensitive man with consumption, who knew the danger of infection, would be a champion spitter.

The Stevensons finally left Sydney on the *Mariposa* on their homeward voyage on 20th March 1893. The ship carried another prominent passenger: the boxer Griffo! Stevenson never returned to Sydney. He was to have another nine fairly happy months, working chiefly on *Weir of Hermiston*, before that fatal evening, on 3rd December, when he collapsed with a cerebral haemorrhage—not tuberculosis—and died. A few weeks earlier he had dictated to Belle the final version of the poem that appears at the beginning of *Weir of Hermiston*. It is addressed to his wife.

> I saw rain falling and the rainbow drawn
> On Lammermuir. Hearkening I heard again
> In my precipitous city beaten bells
> Winnow the keen sea-wind. And here afar,
> Intent on my own race and place, I write.

And so do I!

HER PRIVATES WE

BECAUSE so few Australians today have heard of Frederic Manning or have read his novel *Her Privates We*, there is some danger of exaggerating its obscurity. In fact it was immediately recognized by English critics on its first, shy, anonymous appearance in 1929 under the title of *The Middle Parts of Fortune* by Private 19022, as one of the best books about the First World War, to be compared only with such masterpieces as Robert Graves's *Good-bye to All That*, Siegfried Sassoon's *Memoirs of a Fox-hunting Man* and Edmund Blunden's *Undertones of War*, all of which had already been published. In January 1930 a new edition appeared as *Her Privates We,** still by Private 19022, and was reprinted several times before it was republished under Frederic Manning's name by Peter Davies in 1943. By then Frederic Manning was dead, but his authorship of the book had long been recognized. It was particularly admired

---

* Both these titles, *The Middle Parts of Fortune*, and *Her Privates We*, are taken from the same passage of *Hamlet*:

GUILDENSTERN: On fortune's cap we are not the very button . . .
HAMLET: Then you live about her waist, or in the middle of her favours?
GUILDENSTERN: Faith, her privates, we.

In my own opinion neither title is altogether happy. Both smack of literary cleverness and the pun in *Her Privates We* is wasted on all but Shakespearean scholars.

by such different writers as Arnold Bennett, E. M. Forster and T. E. Lawrence.

It is true that *Her Privates We* was largely ignored at the time in Australia even though its author was an Australian. It is not difficult to guess why. Frederic Manning had become an expatriate. Australians, who are so quick to claim any writer or artist as Australian even if he (or she) was born in another country, are equally quick to disown any Australian born writer who has the temerity to leave Australia. Frederic Manning, who had left the country in 1896 at the age of fourteen in order to be educated in England, was struck off the list of Australian writers even though he never disowned his national origins. His family remained in Australia where his brother, Sir Henry Manning, became Attorney-General of New South Wales, but Frederic's name is dismissed in a few lines in H. M. Green's *A History of Australian Literature*, even though that useful work contains some writers of staggering insignificance. Perhaps it might have been different if Frederic Manning had enlisted in an Australian regiment when war broke out and had written his novel about the Australians at Gallipoli or the Middle East. As it was, he enlisted as a private in the King's Shropshire Light Infantry, and *Her Privates We* is very largely a portrait of the ordinary Englishman at war. But, as I shall try to show later, there is still a good deal that is recognizably Australian in this novel, and it is surely scandalous that it should have been neglected so long in Frederic Manning's native land.

There is however, a more formidable difficulty in bringing this fine novel to the attention of the present generation of Australians. The young today have come to assume that a great book about war must necessarily be a book against war. Their model is that splendid satire *Catch-22* (about which I shall have more to say later) or Norman Mailer's *The Naked and the Dead*. They can hardly conceive that right up to 1914 sensitive and intelligent men like Péguy were still praising war as the noblest human experience. That attitude could not long survive the grim reality of trench warfare, though there are still traces of it in Montherlant's youthful novel *The Dream*. Most of the best books about the First World War were fiercely and rightly critical of the appalling waste of human lives and the obstinate stupidity of the political and military leaders on both sides. One thinks, in particular, of Remarque's *All Quite on the Western Front* and Zweig's *The Case of Sergeant Grischa*. *Her Privates We* is not one of these. It is neither a justification of war—though E. M. Forster thought it was—nor a condemnation of war. It is an acceptance of war as an inevitable part of human experience, an extreme and heightened form of the reality which surrounds us. Manning is not interested in war as a political act but as a crucible in which men are tested. To many people this attitude will now appear inadequate—though it has yet to be proved that Manning is wrong—but it should not be allowed to affect one's judgement of his novel as a work of art.

As Manning wrote in the preface to the novel: "War is waged by men; not by beasts, or by gods. It is a peculiarly human activity. To call it a crime is to miss at least half of its significance; it is also the punishment of a crime. That raises a moral question, the kind of problem with which the present age is disinclined to deal. Perhaps some future attempt to provide a solution for it may prove to be even more astonishing than the last."

Since *Her Privates We* is plainly an autobiographical novel, it may be as well to begin with a few words about the author. Frederic Manning was born in Sydney in 1882, the fourth son of Sir William Patrick Manning. Throughout his life Frederic suffered from ill health—caused chiefly by asthma—and except for six months at Sydney Grammar he was unable to go to school. At the age of fourteen he went to London with Arthur Galton, formerly private secretary to Sir Robert Duff, Governor of New South Wales, and lived with him for some years. It was Galton, a scholarly if slightly eccentric man with a wide knowledge of literature, who introduced him to books and writing.

When he grew up Manning determined to become a writer himself and soon won a modest reputation as a critic, essayist, and poet. His first book of poetry, *The Vigil of Brunhild*, was published in 1907. In the same year he began reviewing books for the *Spectator* and from 1909 to 1914 he was that paper's principal reviewer. In 1909 he also published his first prose work, *Scenes and Portraits*, which consists of imaginary stories and conversations between historical characters. This book was highly praised by Bonamy Dobrée, Max Beerbohm and E. M. Forster, and won him the passionate admiration and later the friendship of T. E. Lawrence. For all its elegance and wit, it now seems precious and artificial, and the prose, consciously based on Pater, somewhat cloying. For our purpose, however, it is important as showing Manning's early preoccupation with the personal, social and political efforts of man to reconcile himself to suffering and death, which is the main theme of *Her Privates We*. In these essays he also reveals his religious attitude which he defined in the preface as follows: "There are in reality only two religions on this little planet and they perhaps begin and end with man. They are: the religion of the humble folk, whose life is a daily communion with the natural forces and a bending to them; and the religion of men like Protgoras, Lucretius, and Montaigne, a religion of doubt, of tolerance and agnosticism. Between these two poles is nothing but a dreary waste of formalism." Manning had a deep respect for the vital religion of "humble folk" but despised formal Christianity. Many years later, in a letter to Sir William Rothenstein, he said that if he had been an orthodox Christian, the war would have shattered his belief, but for him Christianity "is a merely formal symbol".

During those pre-war years Manning seems to have been a rather precious young man, highly intelligent and sensitive, but barred by his delicate health and a certain over-fastidious refinement from any share of common humanity. Peter Davies, his friend and publisher, who later persuaded him to write *Her Privates We*, remembered him as "an intellectual of intellectuals—poet, classical scholar, and author of the exquisite *Scenes and Portraits*—delicate in health and fastidious almost to the point of foppishness". The outbreak of war in 1914 changed his life utterly as it changed the lives of millions of others. In spite of his ill health he felt it his duty to enlist as a private in the ranks of an English County Regiment, the King's Shropshire Light Infantry, refusing a commission on the ground that he had little knowledge of men. He joined his regiment in 1915 and served on the Somme and Ancre fronts in the dreadful year of 1916.

G

Manning survived the war and, immediately after, returned to his chosen life as a writer and scholar. He enjoyed
the friendship of distinguished men like Laurence Binyon,
T. S. Eliot, Richard Aldington and T. E. Lawrence, but seems
to have lived a rather lonely, secretive life. He never married.
He was often too ill to work. However, the great experience
of war was still fermenting in his mind, and eventually Peter
Davies persuaded him to write it down. The result was *Her
Privates We*, a complete break with everything he had done
before. He did not long survive its publication but died of
pneumonia in 1935. T. E. Lawrence (then Aircraftman
Shaw in the Royal Air Force) was on his way to see him when
he heard the news. T. S. Eliot was the only writer present at
his funeral.

Her Privates We is plainly autobiographical. It describes
the experiences of Private Bourne, a soldier in the "Westshires" on the Somme and Ancre fronts, with an interval behind the lines, during the latter half of 1916. Private Bourne,
if not Manning himself, is at least a projection of Manning,
and, though he insisted that the other characters are fictitious,
he added: "It is true that in recording the conversations of the
men I seemed at times to hear the voices of ghosts." It is perhaps worth noting a pardonable slip that reveals the autobiographical nature of the novel: on page 66 of the 1964 edition
(to which all references in this essay will be made) he wrote
that the mare who pulled the mess-cart and (without official
permission) the Lewis gun cart for which Bourne was responsible, "bore no malice, the old lady, as though she knew *we*
had a pretty thin time".

One of the reasons why *Her Privates We* is so successful is
that by making Bourne a man like himself Manning was
able, quite naturally, to make his philosophic comments on
war and the nature of man without interrupting the drive of
the narrative.

The construction of the novel is both simple and admirable. When the book begins, Bourne's battalion is just being
withdrawn from the front line after an attack which has shattered it. The survivors go back behind the lines to rest and
reform—and to prepare for the next offensive which each man
fears will be his death. Each finds in drink or women or

routine tasks the antidote he needs for his overstrung nerves.
Yet hardly have they achieved some normality when they
must again go through the slow, deliberate process of screwing
their courage to the sticking point. For Bourne the next offensive is the last, and the book ends with Sergeant Tozer musing
besides his hideous corpse in the trench:

> It was finished. He was sorry about Bourne, he thought, more
> sorry than he could say. He was a queer chap, he said to him-
> self, as he felt for the dug-out steps. There was a bit of mystery
> about him; but then, when you come to think of it, there's a bit
> of mystery about all of us. He pushed aside the blanket screen-
> ing the entrance, and in the murky light he saw all the men
> lift their faces, and look at him with patient, almost animal
> eyes.

From the beginning the style is direct and vigorous, and the
fourth sentence contains a slang phrase, "beaten to the wide",
which must have come as a shock to those who knew only the
elegant, affected prose of Manning's pre-war books. Throughout the narrative and descriptions of action the sentences are
kept short, terse, and colloquial. It is only when Bourne re-
flects on what is happening around him that Manning permits
himself that more elaborate style which T. E. Lawrence—
and apparently only Lawrence—immediately recognized as
marking the author of *Scenes and Portraits*.

Some of the descriptions of the front are as good as anything ever written about war. Take, for example, this account
of men waiting in the trenches for the barrage to lift before
an attack:

> The drumming of the guns continued, with bursts of great in-
> tensity. It was as though a gale streamed overhead, piling up
> great waves of sound and hurrying them onward to crash in
> surf on the enemy entrenchments. The windless air about them,
> by its very stillness, made that unearthly music more terrible
> to hear. They cowered under it, as men seeking shelter from a
> storm. Something rushed downward on them with a scream of
> exultation, increasing to a roar before it blasted the air asunder
> and sent splinters of steel shrieking over their heads, an erup-
> tion of mud spattering down on the trench, and splashing in
> brimming shell-holes. The pressure among the men increased.
> Someone shouldering a way through caused them to surge to-

gether, cursing, as they were thrown off their balance to stumble against their neighbours.

"For Christ's sake walk on your own bloody feet an' not on mine!" came from some angry man, and a ripple of idiot mirth spread outwards from the centre of the disurbance. Bourne got a drink of tea, and though it was no more than warm, it did him good; at least, it washed away the gummy dryness of his mouth. He was shivering, and told himself it was the cold. Through the darkness the dripping mist moved slowly, touching them with spectral fingers as it passed. Everything was clammy with it. It condensed on their tin hats, clung to their rough serge, their eye-lashes, the down on their cheek-bones. Even though it blinded everything beyond the distance of a couple of yards, it seemed to be faintly luminous itself. Its damp coldness enhanced the sense of smell. There was a reek of mouldering rottenness in the air, and through it came the sour, stale odour from the foul clothes of the men. Shells streamed overhead, sighing, whining and whimpering for blood; the upper air fluttered with them; but Fritz was not going to take it all quietly, and with its increasing roar another shell leaped toward them, and they cowered under the wrath. There was the enormous grunt of its eruption, the sweeping of harp-strings, and part of the trench wall collapsed inwards, burying some men in the landslide. It was difficult to get them out in the crowded conditions of the trench.

Bourne's fit of shakiness increased, until he set his teeth to prevent them chattering in his head; and after a deep, gasping breath, almost like a sob, he seemed to recover to some extent. Fear poisoned the very blood; but, when one recognized the symptoms, it became objective, and one seemed to escape partly from it that way. He heard men breathing irregularly beside him, as he breathed himself; he heard them swallow, as though overcoming a difficulty in swallowing; and the sense that others suffered equally or more than himself, quietened him. Some men moaned, or even sobbed a little, but unconsciously, and as though they struggled to throw off an intolerable burden of oppression. His eyes met Shem's, and they both turned away at once from the dread and question which confronted them. . . .

This was the setting in which hundreds of thousands, even millions of men, lived and struggled and died during those years. This was the reality they all confronted. Yet Manning's interest was not so much in the reality but in how men—

ordinary men without his advantages of education and knowledge—faced this reality. *Her Privates We* is above all a study
of ordinary men in extraordinary conditions. The whole
book is seen from the point of view of the private soldier.
The officers are sketched in only briefly and then as if from a
distance. Bourne, like Manning himself, at first refuses a commission, and is only reluctantly persuaded to put in for one
at the end of the book. Even then he is haunted by feelings of
guilt as though he were betraying his comrades.

Yet Manning is never sentimental about these men. He
looks at them coolly as if they were another race whom he
envies and admires but does not quite understand.

> The simplicity of their outlook on life gave them a certain
> dignity, because it was free from irrelevancies. Certainly they
> had all the appetites of men, and, in the aggregate, probably
> embodied most of the vices to which flesh is prone; but they
> were not preoccupied with their vices and appetites; they could
> master them with rather a splendid indifference; and even
> sensuality has its aspect of tenderness. These apparently rude
> and brutal natures comforted, encouraged, and reconciled each
> other to fate, with a tenderness and tact which was more mov-
> ing than anything in life. They had nothing; not even their
> own bodies, which had become mere implements of warfare.
> They turned from the wreckage and misery of life to an empty
> heaven, and from an empty heaven to the silence of their own
> hearts. They had been brought to the last extremity of hope,
> and yet they put their hands on each other's shoulders and said
> with passionate conviction that it would be all right, though
> they had faith in nothing, but in themselves and in each other.

In *Her Privates We* Manning—or Bourne, for no distinction is possible—continually tries to discover how such men
can face extremes of suffering and the constant threat of death
without breaking. One of the few officers in the book says to
Bourne while sitting together in a dug-out: "You and I are
two of the lucky ones, Bourne; we've come through without
a scratch; and if our luck holds we'll keep moving out of one
bloody misery into another, until we break, see, until we
break." But they don't break. "If a man could not be certain
of himself, he could be certain of nothing. The problem
which confronted them all equally, though some were unable

or unwilling to define it, did not concern death so much as the affirmation of their own will in the face of death; and once the nature of the problem was clearly stated, they realized that its solution was continuous, and could never be final. Death set a limit to the continuance of one factor in the problem, and peace to that of another; but neither of them really affected the nature of the problem itself."

Of course some men *did* break. One of the most moving incidents in the book is the appearance of the deserter, Miller, who runs away before an offensive. He is arrested in Rouen and brought back to the battalion. Manning's treatment of this man and how he is regarded by his comrades seems to me both just and psychologically accurate:

> They were bitter and summary in their judgement on him. The fact that he had deserted his commanding-officer, which would be the phrase used to describe his offence on the charge sheet, was as nothing compared to the fact that he had deserted them. They were to go through it while he saved his skin. It was about as bad as could be, and if one were to ask any man who had been through that spell of fighting what ought to be done in the case of Miller, there could only have been one answer. Shoot the beggar. But if that same man were detailed as one of the firing-party, his feelings would be modified considerably.

Later Miller is paraded before the regiment and his sentence read out.

> He was white and haggard, but his mouth was half-open in an idiotic grin, and the small, furtive eyes wandered restlessly along the line of men drawn up in front of him. Bourne felt a strange emotion rising in him which was not pity but a revulsion from this degradation of a man, who was now only an abject outcast.

I would not wish to suggest that *Her Privates We* is faultless. Manning's strength lay in description and philosophical analysis. He was not naturally endowed with a gift for creating character or for dialogue. I confess that I find much of the dialogue in *Her Privates We* false and unconvincing. Here, of course, some caution is necessary. It is extremely difficult, writing in 1971, to be sure exactly how either officers or men spoke in 1916. Manning makes most of the men talk in a kind of simple dialect which, I suppose, is meant to represent the speech of the men in the King's Shropshire Light Infantry. I was at school at Shrewsbury and, while I do not pretend to be an expert, I do not recognize their speech as particularly characteristic. (Again one must be careful. In the First as well as the Second World wars territorial recruiting soon broke down. Manning makes it clear that the Westshires included miners from the Midlands as well as countrymen from Shropshire. In the Second World War my own battalion of the King's Own Scottish Borderers had many miners from Durham—and very good soldiers they were.) He is equally open to criticism when he ventures to put speech into the mouths of Scots soldiers from the Gordon's. Would a Highlander then—or now—have said: "Gude day t' ye, an' gude luck, chums"? But even Bourne himself, who should have been easier for Manning, often sounds false. Would he really have spoken to his fellow soldiers like this: "Don't let us go back to kip yet, sergeant. . . . Let us go a little way behind the huts, and sit down, and smoke and talk. It is such a ripping night. Look at that slag-heap over there, cutting the sky-line like the Rock of Gibraltar. There's another towards Sains. The wine has enlivened without exciting me?" Or this: "The question of right in this connection is of merely academic interest, . . . but you would admit that we have a prior claim, and therefore are in a stronger position than you are. I am not going to conceal from you, Humphreys, the fact that your presence is unwelcome to us." And if he had done, would he have been accepted by the men as Bourne was accepted? I cannot think so.

I think it must also be admitted that, apart from Bourne himself, most of the other characters are shadowy. They are perfectly distinct, recognizable, human beings, but they lack both depth and vividness. Bourne's own particular friends— the boy Martlow, Shem, Sergeant Tozer—never quite come to life. There is one exception to this. Towards the end of the book he introduces another character, Weeper Smart, who is wholly and fiercely alive. Weeper Smart is not an attractive character and is not meant to be. He is tall and strong but cadaverous and ugly, and his soul is consumed with raging bitterness against the war, the army, the officers and life itself.

Manning uses him cleverly to express the men's resentment against the miseries of life in the trenches, the futility of parades, and the stupidity of orders from above. He is one of the very few characters in the book who openly express scepticism about the purpose of the war.

> "We're fightin' for all we've bloody got," said Madely bluntly.
> "An' that's sweet F.A.," said Weeper Smart. "A tell thee, that all a want to do is to save me own bloody skin. An' the first thing a do, when a go into t' line, is to find out where t' bloody dressing-stations are; an' if a can get a nice blighty, chaps, when once me face is turned towards home, I'm laughing. You won't see me bloody arse for dust. A'm not proud. A tell thee straight. Them as thinks different can 'ave all the bloody war they want, and me own share of it, too."

There, in different accents, speaks the voice of Yossarian in *Catch-22*. But there is a difference. Joseph Heller is entirely on the side of Yossarian. He is Yossarian as Manning is Bourne. But Manning/Bourne is not on the side of Weeper Smart. He recognizes his strength, his intelligence, his individuality, but he is not on his side. He is on the side of the men who endure without complaining. Yet something slowly draws Bourne and Weeper Smart together in a curious friendship.

> No one could have had a greater horror and dread of war than Weeper had. It was a continuous misery to him, and yet he endured it. Living with him, one felt instinctively he would not let one down, that he had in him, curiously, an heroic strain: Martlow, who had been brought up to read people's characters, said of him that he would be just as bloody miserable in peacetime; and perhaps he was right. Bourne, contrasting the two men, decided that Weeper's defect lay in being too imaginative, when it flashed on his mind that while his imagination tortured him with apprehension, it was actually his strength.

It is Weeper Smart who volunteers to go with Bourne on that last fatal patrol between the lines, even though he despises volunteering, just because he thinks Bourne has been

treated unjustly. And it is Weeper Smart who goes back to
him when Bourne is hit.

> Weeper turned his head over his shoulder, listened, stopped,
> and went back. He found Bourne trying to lift himself; and
> Bourne spoke, gasping, suffocating.
> "Go on, I'm scuppered."
> "A'll not leave thee," said Weeper. . . .
> He felt Bourne stretch himself in a convulsive shudder, and
> relax, becoming suddenly heavier in his arms. He struggled
> on, stumbling over the shell-ploughed ground through that
> fantastic mist, which moved like an army of wraiths, hurrying
> away from him. Then he stopped, taking the body by the waist
> with his left arm, flung it over his shoulder, steadying it with
> his right. He could see their wire now, and presently he was
> challenged, and replied. He found the way through the wire,
> and staggered into the trench with his burden. Then he turned
> down the short stretch of Delaunay to Mank Trench, and came
> on the rest of the party outside A Company's dug-out.
> "A've brought 'im back," he cried desperately, and collapsed
> with the body on the duck-boards. Picking himself up again,
> he told his story incoherently, mixed with raving curses.
> "What are you gibbering about?" said Sergeant Morgan.
> " 'aven't you ever seen a dead man before?"

Why didn't Manning side with Weeper Smart? This brings
us squarely to the central question of Manning's attitude to
war. I do not think that this question would have worried
many readers in 1930 when, in spite of the revulsion against
the First World War, most people still accepted that wars
were inevitable and that it was a man's duty to fight and die
for his country. Today a new generation is growing up which
questions both these things. Their view is expressed most brilliantly in Heller's *Catch-22*, undoubtedly the greatest book
to come out of the Second World War and one of the greatest
satires in English and American literature. For that reason I
have found it instructive to compare *Catch-22* with *Her
Privates We*. There are, of course, many obvious differences
between these two great books. *Catch-22* is a brilliantly funny
satire; *Her Privates We* a deeply serious book with only occasional passages of comedy. *Catch-22* is about the American
Air Force; *Her Privates We* about the British Army. Enlisted

men are almost as rare and shadowy characters in *Catch-22* as officers in *Her Privates We*. Yet essentially they are about the same things. Both books are concerned with suffering and death.

Heller/Yossarian, as is well known, thinks the war is insane, a monstrous conspiracy against life in general and his own in particular. At times he sounds selfish—and remarkably like Weeper Smart:

> Clevinger knew everything about the war except why Yossarian had to die while Corporal Snark was allowed to live, or why Corporal Snark had to die while Yossarian was allowed to live. It was a vile and muddy war, and Yossarian could have lived without it—lived forever, perhaps. Only a fraction of his countrymen would give up their lives to win it, and it was not his ambition to be among them. To die or not to die, that was the question, and Clevinger grew limp trying to answer it. History did not demand Yossarian's premature demise, justice could be satisfied without it, progress would not hinge upon it, victory did not depend on it. That men would die was a matter of necessity; *which* men would die, though, was a matter of circumstance, and Yossarian was willing to be the victim of anything but circumstance. But that was war.

Manning/Bourne, on the other hand, accepts from the first that death is inevitable and that to die in war is not necessarily the worst thing that can happen. He expresses this first, in phrases consciously echoing Shakespeare, through the mouth of Sergeant Tozer:

> "You know, to my way o' thinkin' some of us'ns 'ave a dam' sight more religion than some o' the parsons who preach at us. We're willin' to take a chance, we are. 'uman nature's 'uman nature, an' you may be right or you may be wrong, but if you bloody well think you're right, you may as well get on with it. What does it matter if y'are killed? You've got to die some day. You've got to chance your arm in this life, an' a dam' sight more than your arm too sometimes. Some folk talk a lot about war bein' such a bloody waste; but I'm not so sure it's such a bloody waste after all. . . . Do they think we came out for seven bloody bob a week? I'm not troublin' about my bloody conscience. I've got some self respect, I 'ave."

Bourne appreciated Sergeant Tozer's point of view, because

he understood the implications his words were intended to convey, even when he seemed to wander from the point. Life was a hazard enveloped in mystery [did Churchill remember that phrase?] and war quickened the sense of both in men: the soldier also, as well as the saint, might write his tractate de contemptu mundi, and differ from him only in the angle and spirit from which he surveyed the same bleak reality.

Later Manning/Bourne admits that

Whether it were justified or not, however, the sense of being at the disposal of some inscrutable power, using them for its own ends, and utterly indifferent to them as individuals, was perhaps the most tragic element in the men's present situation. It was not much use telling them that war was only the ultimate problem of all human life stated barely, and pressing for an immediate solution. When each individual conscience cried out for its freedom, that implacable thing said: "Peace, peace; your freedom is only in me!" Men recognized the truth intuitively, even with their reason checking at a fault. There was no man of them unaware of the mystery which encompassed him, for he was a part of it; he could neither separate himself entirely from it, nor identify himself with it completely. A man might rave against war; but war, from among its myriad faces, could always turn him one, which was his own. All this resentment against officers, against authority, meant very little, even to the men themselves. It fell away from them in words.

It would be unfair to regard the first quotation from *Catch-22* as expressing Heller/Yossarian's total view. Yossarian proves both by his words and actions that he is deeply compassionate. He also comes to see that war, with its urgent and immediate threat of death, is only an intensification of the myriad threats that always surround life. In this respect he is very like Manning/Bourne. But whereas Heller/Yossarian thinks that "the point is to keep them from dying for as long as you can", Manning/Bourne thinks that the point is to die as well as you can. Both writers put their thoughts into a discussion between their characters: In *Her Privates We* the men are discussing an order forbidding soldiers advancing into action from stopping to help the wounded:

"There's nought sure for us'ns, anyway," said Weeper, relaps-
ing. "Dids't 'ear what Cap'n Thompson read out this mornin',
about stoppin' to 'elp any poor beggar what was wounded?
The bloody brass-'at what wrote that letter 'as never been in
any big show 'isself, that a dare swear. 'e's one o' them muckers
as is never nearer to the real thing than G.H.Q."

"You don't want to talk like that," said Corporal Hamley.
"You've 'ad your orders."

"A don't mind tellin' thee, corporal," said Weeper, again
lifting a large, flat hand as though by that gesture he stopped
the mouths of all the world. "A don't mind tellin' thee, that if
a see a chum o' mine down, an' a can do aught to 'elp 'im, all
the brass-'ats in the British Army, 'an there's a bloody sight too
many o' 'em, aren't goin' to stop me. A'll do what's right, an'
if a know aught about thee, thal't do as A do. . . . They don't
know what we've to go through, that's the truth of it," said
Weeper. "They measure the distance, an' they count the men,
an' the guns, an' think a battle's no but a sum you can do wi' a
pencil an' a bit o' paper. . . ."

"Give them a chance," said Bourne reasonably; he hadn't
spoken before, he usually sat back and listened quietly to these
debates.

"Let 'em take my bloody chance!" shouted Weeper, vindic-
tively.

"There's a good deal in what you say," said Bourne, who was
a little embarrassed by the way they all looked at him suddenly. "I think there's a good deal of truth in it; but after all,
what is a brass-hat's job? He's not thinking of you or of me or
of any individual man, or of any particular battalion or
division. Men, to him, are only part of the material he has got
to work with; and if he felt as you or I feel, he couldn't carry
on with his job. It's not fair to think he's inhuman. . . . Once
we go over the top it's the colonel's and the company com-
mander's job. Once we meet a Hun it's our job. . . ."

"Yes, an' our job's a bloody sight worse'n theirs," said
Weeper.

In *Catch-22* the officers are discussing an order to go and
bomb Bologna—a particularly dreaded target:

Clevinger agreed with ex-P.F.C. Wintergreen that it was Yossarian's job to get killed over Bologna and was livid with
condemnation when Yossarian confessed that it was he who

had moved the bomb-line and caused the mission to be cancelled.

"Why the hell not?" Yossarian snarled, arguing all the more vehemently because he suspected he was wrong. "Am I supposed to get my ass shot off just because the colonel wants to be a general?"

"What about the men on the mainland?" Clevinger demanded with just as much emotion. "Are they supposed to get their asses shot off just because you don't want to go? Those men are entitled to air support!"

"But not necessarily by me. Look, they don't care who knocks out those ammunition dumps. The only reason we're going is because that bastard Cathcart volunteered us."

"Oh I know all that," Clevinger assured him. . . . "But it's not for us to determine what targets must be destroyed or who's to destroy them or. . . ."

"Or who gets killed doing it? And why?"

"Yes, even that. We have no right to question—"

"You're insane!"

"—no right to question—"

"Do you really mean that it's not my business how or why I get killed and that it is Colonel Cathcart's? Do you really mean that?"

"Yes, I do," Clevinger insisted, seeming unsure. "There are men entrusted with winning the war who are in a much better position than we are to decide what targets have to be bombed."

"We are talking about two different things," Yossarian answered with exaggerated weariness. "You are talking about the relationship of the Air Corps to the infantry, and I am talking about the relationship of me to Colonel Cathcart. You are talking about winning the war, and I am talking about winning the war and keeping alive."

"Exactly," Clevinger snapped smugly. "And which do you think is more important?"

"To whom?" Yossarian shot back. "Open your eyes, Clevinger. It doesn't make a damned bit of difference *who* wins the war to someone who's dead."

But perhaps the greatest difference between the two authors is in their attitude to the phenomenon of war. Heller/Yossarian regards it as a lunatic interruption to life which can benefit only cruel, selfish and corrupt men. A wise man (like Yossarian) will try to get out of the fighting; a wise country (like Italy) will try to be defeated. Manning/Bourne, on the other hand, deeply influenced by history and literature of the past, regards war as an inevitable part of human destiny.

> "C'est la guerre", they would say, with resignation that was almost apathy: for all sensible people know that war is one of the blind forces of nature, which can neither be foreseen nor controlled. Their attitude, in all its simplicity, was sane. There is nothing in war which is not in human nature; but the violence and passions of men become, in the aggregate, an impersonal and incalculable force, a blind and irrational movement of the collective will, which one cannot control, which one cannot understand, which one can only endure as these peasants, in their bitterness and resignation, endured it. C'est la guerre.

Starting from this point of view Manning could see in war nobility and even ecstasy, "transfiguring all the circumstances of life so that these could only be expressed in the terms of heroic tragedy, of some superhuman or even divine conflict with the powers of evil". Starting from his point of view Heller could see only cruelty, corruption and death. There will be many people today who will think that, in this nuclear age, Heller is right and Manning wrong, but this does not detract from the nobility and dignity of Manning's vision. He is, after all, closer to Shakespeare and to Homer than is Heller.

Finally, I wish to deal with the complaint, sometimes raised, that *Her Privates We* has nothing to do with Australia and can therefore be ignored by Australians. I do not think it is a serious charge, for Manning was dealing with universal themes which should be of as much interest to Australians as to anyone else. However, it is not even true. There are many proofs of Manning's Australian origins and outlook in this book. Let us take the more trivial ones first. On page 9 Manning describes how Bourne dodges the Prussian machine-gunners:

> They were singularly brave men, these Prussian machine-gunners, but the extreme of heroism, alike in foe or friend, is in-

distinguishable from despair. Bourne found himself playing again a game of his childhood, though not now among rocks from which reverberated heat quivered in wavy films, but in made fissures too chalky and unweathered for adequate concealment.

He is certainly not talking of England! On page 58 he describes his isolation from the men in his battalion:

He was not of their county, he was not even of their country, or their religion, and he was only partially of their race. When they spoke of their remote villages and hamlets, or sleepy market-towns in which nothing happened except the church clock chiming the hour, he felt an alien among them; and in the vague kind of home-sickness which troubled him he did not seek company, but solitude.

On page 181 Bourne's friend Martlow pokes fun at him for using bad language.

"Oh, you all swear like so many Eton boys," replied Bourne, indifferently. "Have you ever heard an Aussie swear?" "No, 'n I don't want," said Martlow. "Them beggars 'ave too much spare cash to know what soldierin' means."

On the march to Louvencourt (page 208) "they passed an Australian driving a horse-drawn lorry, with a heavy load whereon he sprawled, smoking a cigarette with an indolence which Bourne envied. The Colonel wheeled his grey, and pursued him with a fire of invective practically the whole length of the column, to the man's obvious amazement, as he had never before been told off at such length, and with such fluent vigour, in language to which no lady could take exception. He sat up, and got rid of his cigarette, looking both innocent and perplexed." Later one of the men mentions this incident. " 'You want a few thousand Australians in the British Army,' said Bourne angrily. 'They would put the wind up some of these bloody details who think they own the earth.' "

All these extracts seem to prove conclusively that not only did Manning feel that he was an Australian when he was writing the book but that he wished Bourne to be recognized as an Australian. However, that is not the end of the matter. It seems to me undeniable that there is something very Australian in Bourne's attitude to discipline and rank as described by Manning. It would be absurd to pretend that there were no democrats in the British Army in the First World War— though they were probably rarer than in the Second—but Bourne is democratic in a peculiarly Australian way. Very early he comes to the conclusion that "there was too much bloody discipline in the British Army". He is infuriated by pointless distinctions between ranks, especially behind the lines, and one of the few really bitter passages is that in which he finds that champagne and other delicacies in the Expeditionary Force Canteen are reserved for officers.

> "If I were a colonel," said Bourne; "mind you, only a colonel; and a man like that bloody lance-jack, who has never even smelt a dead horse in South Africa, turned one of my men out of a canteen started for the benefit of the troops by public subscription, I would get the battalion together, and I would sack the whole bloody institution from basement to garret, even if I were to be broke for it."

One likes to think that there were, and still are, Australian colonels who would have done just that.

Bourne's reluctance to accept a commission and his feeling that, if he does, he will be betraying his mates, is also typically Australian. I have met Australians who took precisely this attitude in the Second World War.

Finally, there is a passage which I do not think has been noticed before. In it Bourne is describing his relationship with the men to the chaplain, who has asked him if he has any friends among them.

> Bourne paused for quite an appreciable time.
> "No," he said finally. "I don't suppose I have anyone, whom I can call a friend. I like the men, on the whole, and I think they like me. They're a very decent generous lot, and they have helped me a great deal. I have one or two particular chums, of course; and in some ways, you know, good comradeship takes the place of friendship. It is different: it has its own loyalties and affections; and I am not sure that it does not rise on occasion to an intensity of feeling which friendship never touches. It may be less in itself, I don't know, but it's opportunity is greater. Friendship implies rather more stable conditions, don't

HER PRIVATES WE 103

you think? You have time to choose. Here you can't choose, or only to a very limited extent. I didn't think heroism was such a common thing. I have seen a man risking himself for another more than once: I don't say they would all do it. It seems to me to be a spontaneous and irreflective action, like the kind of start forward you make instinctively when you see a child playing in a street turn and run suddenly almost under a car. At one moment a particular man may be nothing at all to you, and the next minute you will go through hell for him. No, it is not friendship. The man doesn't matter so much, it's a kind of impersonal emotion, a kind of enthusiasm, in the old sense of the word. Of course one is keyed-up, a bit overwrought. We help each other. What is one man's fate today, may be another's to-morrow. We are all in it up to the neck together, and we know it."

Is not this the best description of "mateship" ever written? Today "mateship" is unfashionable, and some writers even deny that such a thing ever existed in Australia. That is nonsense. It existed for precisely the same reason that it existed among Bourne's comrades—because in the harsh conditions of early settlement men couldn't choose their friends; they were all in it up to the neck together. In these circumstances comradeship or mateship does take the place of friendship, and I think that Manning knew this instinctively where an Englishman—or at least a middle-class, educated Englishman—might not. And it is this recognition and understanding which makes *Her Privates We* one of the most sympathetic accounts of soldiers at war that has ever been written.

H

ETHEL ANDERSON

IF I were asked who is Australia's best prose writer, I would name Ethel Anderson. Since this may cause some derision among those who have never heard of her or, if they have, know her only as an excellent but minor poet, I will explain more precisely what I mean. I do not mean, of course, that Ethel Anderson is a greater novelist than, say, Patrick White or Randolph Stow or Henry Handel Richardson. That would be absurd. Ethel Anderson never wrote a novel, and, if she had done, she would not have attempted the higher flights of that genre. Her own field was the short story, the *conte*, in which her wit, her gift for lyrical description and her idiosyncratic sense of comedy could best be displayed.

What I do mean is that in the best of these tales her prose style reached a more sensitive and disciplined pitch of perfection than that of any other Australian writer. Since even this claim may seem a bit far-fetched to the unconverted, I will begin by quoting three short passages from *At Parramatta*, her best work, each of which, I believe, shows a different facet of her art.

The first quotation consists of the first two paragraphs from the first chapter. It is designed not only to introduce one of the main characters but to set the tone for the whole book.

Dr Phantom did not really care for children. It is doubtful whether any child had ever been invited to ride beside him in the dashing Hyde Park in which he made his daily rounds. This was a canopied and curtained vehicle, its four wheels rimmed with iron, and it was drawn by a pie-bald Waler, and driven by a white-gloved personable murderer.

It was usual in those days for citizens of Sydney who applied for convict servants to ask for a murderer if any should happen to be available. They were in great demand, for, though apt to be impulsive on occasions of emotion, killers had generally been found to have warmer-hearted and more likeable dispositions than criminals of other persuasions. Dr Phantom, caring little for thieves, sheepstealers, pickpockets, lags, or the abductors of heiresses, employed, when he could do so, only murderers. Though he drew the line at poisoners (his dispensary being, he felt, a temptation) he was at this period particularly lucky; he was rich in the possession of 'First and Second Murderers'—as he designated them—and his servants' hall, in the neat red-brick Georgian house, some twenty miles from the capital, had never been more cheery.

The second quotation describes the special brew of Nyppa Wine (made from a recipe handed down by an ancestor who had been a nabob in Calcutta) with which the vicar's wife, Mrs McCree, hoped—as it proved in vain—to intoxicate the Bishop:

The liquor was chilled to that clammy yet inviting coldness that only the deep-delved earth can give. Its colour was not bright but treacherous-looking; it had the unsafe look of a bog, strangely unluminous, yet deep-toned. It did not seem to be inanimate! Continually, a kind of subterranean glow radiated from it, its surface would be sucked in, in a thousand dimples, and then, with a sort of sucking sound, released, to flow to the rim of the jug. A volcano that was not in eruption but which was brewing lava would perhaps be a simile that faintly hinted at its mysterious and peculiar qualities; it appeared to be as thick as treacle, but it wasn't! As for its bouquet!

The third quotation, an example of Ethel Anderson's elegant and scholarly wit, describes the vicar's wife herself:

The Vicar's wife was convinced that though St Paul might possibly be an inspiration to saints and martyrs, who need not of course, be people of much social standing, only the classics, only Horace, could create a gentleman. Mrs McCree had no use for "Nature's gentlemen". Indeed, she was really desolate that there had not been, that there never could have been, an Epistle from Horace to St Paul.

Having thus, I hope, substantiated my claim or at least roused the interest of sceptics, I can deal with Ethel Anderson's prose works a little more fully. For a beautiful prose style by itself is insufficient. A writer must have something to say or some personal vision to share. It is my contention that Ethel Anderson, through her delicate mixture of wit and poetry, her highly individual and fantastic comedy which reminds one a little of Ronald Firbank* (whom she greatly admired), contributed something unique to Australian literature. It is a scandal that she should already be in danger of being utterly forgotten.

Although Ethel Anderson (née Ethel Louise Mason) was born in Leamington, England, in 1883, she was a fifth generation Australian. Both her parents were Australian and she was brought up and educated first at Picton, in New South Wales, and then at Sydney. When still a young girl, however, she married Austin Thomas Anderson, a British officer serving in the Indian Army, and left Australia to live with him, first in India and then (after the First World War) in England. She did not return to Australia until her husband retired from the Army in 1926. This was unwise because Australians, as I said earlier, are quick to disown any Australian writer who has the temerity to live overseas.

Ethel Anderson then compounded her error. It was bad enough to marry a British officer who rose to the rank of Brigadier General. It was worse still when her husband, on coming to Australia, was appointed to the staff of three successive Governors of New South Wales (Sir Dudley de Chair, Sir Philip Game and Sir Alexander Hore-Ruthven) and finally Private Secretary and Comptroller to the Governor-General, Lord Gowrie. Australians could not believe that anyone who spent much of her social life in and around Govern-

---

* In a letter written to me on 15th Nov. 1957, Ethel Anderson said: "I think I would have *died* without Ronald Firbank when first we returned: I have studied him!"

ment House could be a serious writer (she was), let alone that, when her husband died in 1949, she might have to write for a living (she did).

To some extent Ethel Anderson's own manner tended to confirm this misconception of her as an aristocratic grande dame. Those who visited her in her old age at Turramurra, as I did, found her a delightful, amusing, but somewhat formidable old lady. She sat in a drawing-room surrounded by bric-à-brac collected in India and flourishing an immense silver ear-trumpet—she was very deaf—like the trunk of an elephant. She used this instrument rather in the same way as Billy Hughes is alleged to have used his hearing aid. When she was tired of listening to you, and wanted to talk herself (which was most of the time), she simply removed the trumpet from her ear and switched you off. But her conversation was witty, erudite and very much to the point.

She was neither sweet nor gentle, the two adjectives usually reserved for old ladies. Though she adored her own friends and family, she did not waste time in any general but vague affection for the human race, and she was able to regard its sufferings with equanimity. I think this emerges from her writing. Her Indian tales reveal no sympathy for the toiling masses or her Australian tales for the convicts. Perhaps only Ethel Anderson could have permitted one of her characters, Dr Phantom, to remark, on observing the Rector entering Mrs Furbelow's lean-to: "the latest addition to the poor widow's family of twenty is about to pass, non-stop, through this vale of tears".

But her dedication to the art of writing was professional, thorough and absolute. She was a considerable scholar, knowing a little Greek and a lot of Latin. She was well read in French as well as English literature and especially admired Verlaine, Lamartine, Violette le Duc and—significantly—Colette. There is a good deal of Colette in her own sensuous descriptions of fruit and flowers and wine. She was also, though this is incidental, an accomplished pianist, a keen amateur painter and a discerning critic of contemporary art.

Ethel Anderson always considered herself a poet rather than a prose writer, and it was as a poet that she made what reputation she enjoyed during her lifetime. But it is plain that she also worked hard to improve and develop her prose style, as can easily be seen by studying her four published works. The first, *Adventures in Appleshire*, appeared in Sydney in 1944 (six of the stories had already appeared in the *Sydney Morning Herald*). They are rather slight, charming sketches about her life in Warwickshire in England where she and her husband lived for a time after the First World War. Today they seem a little dated, a trifle Angela Thirkellish, with their cosy gossip about servants and the local hunt ball. But they already reveal her talent for lyrical description of flowers and fruit and trees, her amused observation of human foibles and, in one story, "Hold Gold", the first signs of that fantastic comedy which was to prove her true *métier*.

Her second book, *Indian Tales*, published in 1948, is much stronger. They are all stories about north India, some based on her own experiences as the wife of an officer serving on the frontier, others based on historical incidents in the history of India. (After her death another collection of Indian tales was published under the title *Little Ghosts*. This contains five of the stories from *Indian Tales* but also nine new ones. Since, however, I suspect that most, if not all these, were written about the time she wrote *Indian Tales*, I propose to discuss them together.)

It can be argued, perhaps, that these stories too are marred by a rather old-fashioned attitude towards India and Indians for which the young wife of a British officer before the First World War could be forgiven but will hardly pass now. She had a great admiration for the Hindu Rajputs and their wives and for those peoples whom the British used to call "the warrior castes". For the rest of India's millions she seems to have little interest, and her treatment of Eurasians is at times uncharitable and even offensive. In spite of this defect, however, several of the Indian tales are extremely well written, and three of them, "Chess with Akbar", "Mrs James Greene" and "Twenty-four Elephants", are something more. "Chess with Akbar" is an imaginative account, based on historical evidence, of the Emperor Akbar's last game of chess at Fatehpur Sikhri in which the chess-men were living men and women. ("In changing their squares the slave girls stretched their arms above their heads, laced their finger-tips together, and rotated till their skirts were spinning waist-high; they sank down in the posture called 'lotus-bud asleep'.")

"Mrs James Greene" is something of an oddity. It is an extremely powerful story, again based on historical evidence, of the young wife of Cornet Greene of the Green Bays, who was murdered with his fellow officers by the Sowars of his regiment on the first day of the Indian Mutiny. Mrs Greene with a few other women and an old man escaped the massacre of civilians which followed immediately only to fall into the hands of a local rajah who decided to gamble his prisoners in a cock-fight. Mrs Greene's beauty and courage—she was only sixteen though she had a baby son—won the admiration of a young Sowar in her husband's regiment who was present. Mrs Greene had been kind to his own wife when her first child was born. The Sowar rescued Mrs Greene, hid her in his own house in Sitapur, and sheltered her there until the Mutiny was over. All her companions were killed.

Mrs Greene never left the Sowar's house. Slowly, against her will, she fell in love with him. He had already been stirred by her youthful beauty.

It was on the sixth spring of her sojourn under Mirza Khan's roof that Mrs Greene hung up on the bough of her pipul tree the tinsel swing garlanded with champak flowers, and spread out on the smooth lawn of her garden the sweet-scented couch of love, the quilt of neem flowers and jasmines, the neatly arranged rows of frangipanni blossoms, and waited for Mirza Khan to visit her.

Nearly forty years later an English traveller, walking through a bazaar in a remote Punjab village, had his attention caught by the vivid blue eyes of an old beggar woman who was leading by the hands a blind old man, a very stately, white-bearded figure, soldierly and dignified.

The traveller stopped the woman and asked if she was not English. After a little she admitted it and, when asked her name, replied, "Mrs James Greene—spelt with an 'E'."

The oddity of this story which, as H. M. Green rightly says in his *History of Australian Literature*, "comes near being a masterpiece", is that it is quite different from any other of

Ethel Anderson's stories. It contains none of her wit and humour, very little of her poetry and lyrical description. It is a plain tale told with great power and restraint. It suggests that Ethel Anderson could have achieved success in quite a different style from the one she chose, but perhaps she herself knew that she could not sustain it. Even so, I do not know a better short story in Australian literature.

The third Indian Tale which deserves mention is the delightful, bitter-sweet, "Twenty-four Elephants" in which, I believe, she first discovered and brought to perfection her true talent. (I am assuming, of course, that it was written before, not after, *At Parramatta*.) Once again this is based on a real historical character, Sir David Ochterlony, a Scotsman who served the East India Company in Oudh towards the beginning of the eighteenth century. Sir David lived like an Indian prince and, like an Indian prince, had his own harem or High Seraglio, though this was not a term Sir David himself cared to hear used. He merely said "ma hoose", or referred to its inmates as "ma wee lassies" or even "the leddies".

Every evening, as their sole recreation, "the leddies" were packed into the howdahs of twenty-four elephants for their evening excursion "to eat the air".

> The third elephant carried the Princess Arnawaz, a Persian, her two sons, her "confidential friends", the ladies Farida and Nahid, and two concubines. These ladies might be called the smart set or even the fast set of the household they adorned. Their dark and flashing eyes were rimmed with kohl. Their cheeks were painted with ceruse. Their bare waists were as supple as a flue of silk. Their nails were stained to a beautiful red with arkhanda. Their unveiled loveliness (for they were Persians) shamed the thirty-six stars called Wujah. So lovely were they that while their lackeys shouted "Band! Band! Make way for the Princess Arnawaz!" their ayahs squatted on the roadway and burnt rue to keep off demons, and all the bystanders exclaimed "Wah! Wah!" These resplendent beings moved off on the young elephant, So Sorry Cannot Wait, who was panoplied in blue and silver.

One evening one of the elephants does not return. Sir David, informed of this by an Indian boy who has the unusual ability to count to twenty-six, summons a meeting of his women in the Grand Seraglio and holds an inquiry. He quickly discovers that the Princess Arnawaz and her attendant ladies are missing—and also that they are all enceinte. Later he receives a pathetic message, together with a present of grapes from Khorasan. The letter ran as follows:

"Beloved,
"We, unworthy women, wounded to the marrow of the heart, left the felicity of Your Honour's protection, and wilfully deprived ourselves of the sunbeams radiating from the warmth of Your Magnificence, because we, unworthy vessels, wished our promised children, should they be daughters, to be allowed to live."

Only then did Sir David realize that the Dowager, the Begum Miriam (rigorously schooled in the harem of the Emperor Aurangzeb) and Usbeg the Persian (the Keeper of the High Seraglio), so highly recommended to him by Shah Shuja (who had written of him, "He is economical and orthodox extremely,") had been, as it is called, "old-fashioned" in their rule of his household. Following the ancient custom of the country, the Begum Miriam and Usbeg the Persian had allowed no girl-babies to survive the moment of birth.

But it was in *At Parramatta*, published in Sydney in 1956, that Ethel Anderson's gifts reached their maturity. This book is not quite a collection of short stories and not quite a novel. All the stories are set in or near Parramatta at the time of the Crimean War and the same characters appear in each. Though each story stands on its own, there is some development both of character and plot. Girls grow up, fall in love, marry and have babies. There is a certain vagueness about time, but we are told in the second chapter that the Reverend Phineas McCree is eighty-four and by the last chapter he is ninety-nine! That suggests an elapse of fifteen years, though his grandson, Donalbain, is four years old in the second chapter and "in his last term at the King's School" in the last, which suggests a shorter period. We are told repeatedly that "the Crimean War was not yet over"; since the Crimean war lasted only from 1854 to 1856, time seems to have moved more slowly in Parramatta than in Europe!

There are also some minor historical errors. "Blackbirding", to which there are two references, did not begin until

1863. More serious, perhaps, the system of assigning convicts to private employers was brought to an end in 1841, so Dr Phantom could not have got his First and Second Murderers in 1854. But it would be quite wrong to take *At Parramatta* as a historical novel or a piece of social realism. One does not read *Cardinal Pirelli* to get an accurate picture of the Catholic Church in Spain in the nineteenth century. One does not recommend *Prancing Nigger* to students of the socio-historical development of Haiti. *At Parramatta* is a fantastic comedy which Ethel Anderson used to express her own love of the Australian countryside as well as her highly developed sense of human absurdity. When Mrs McCree looks across the fields towards the Razorback and recalls her childhood in the Picton hills, she is voicing Ethel Anderson's own childhood memories. When Ethel Anderson describes, with her usual accurate detail, the uniform of the Bombay Horse Artillery and notes that the horsehair streamers, which had then replaced the old ostrich feathers on their brass helmets, "could stand up to the most brisk engagement", whereas the High Command had found that "during a long, hot battle, the feathers lost their curl", she is drawing on her own rich experience of military nonsense.

Real blood and real suffering do not appear in these stories. The only violence is a battle, fought with pumpkins and melons, at the Parramatta Royal Horticultural Show. Indeed evil is allowed to appear only once, in the remarkable story of Donalbain and the ducklings, though there is never the least doubt that Ethel Anderson recognized it when she saw it. *At Parramatta* belongs rather to the world of Shakespeare's *Midsummer Night's Dream* or Iris Murdoch's novels. Girls are mated and married off with ridiculous celerity when it suits their author's whim. A man has only to look at a girl to fall madly in love with her. It is a curious mixture of farce and fairyland.

Yet—and this is one of the qualities that make Ethel Anderson unique—all the images and metaphors are precise, accurate and often earthy. If this is not a real world it is a world of real things. Ethel Anderson never wrote of peaches; they were Jargonells or Bergamots; nor of pears, they were Golden Pears of Xaintonge or Beurré du Roi ("Yes, I thought I could not be mistaken! The skin paler than the finest champagne! The shape, symmetrical, but slightly squat, if one could apply so bald a word to so desirable a form! Pipless! Indeed the faultless fruit.") Sometimes her passion for accuracy leads almost to pedantry. Lesser writers might describe a young woman's tantrums as being worthy of a great actress. Ethel Anderson despises such vagueness: "Mrs Siddons as Lady Macbeth, Malabran as Desdemona, Wilhelmina Schroder-Devrient as Leonora, Pauline Viardot-Garcia as Orpheus, though (to heighten the pathos) they would have worn tights (except, perhaps, Lady Macbeth), even in their greatest hour could never have raised such a tempest of emotion as Babette did now, pouring out a torrent of words in an unknown tongue. She was superb."

Throughout the book one is continually surprised and delighted by the vivid, precise phrase. "The Vicarage buckboard, an unwired aviary of chirping girls, and drawn with cloppy animation by 'old' Ruby, who was rising two, then set off, to creak, to hesitate, to side-slip in the ruts of the sandy track that led from Mallow's Marsh to Lanterloo Bay." "The punt slapped and staggered its way across the surging river." What good writing that is! How fresh and admirable! And the wit is pervasive, delicate, ironic and slightly acidulous. It is difficult to choose examples from so much richness—my object, after all, is to make you read the book yourself—but here are two:

Fragrance, his first-born, was Mr Thistledew's favourite. Mrs Thistledew, with infinite tact keeping the less pleasant facts of life from him, as much as possible, hid her other girls very carefully in the background; it is really doubtful whether her husband guessed that he had more than four daughters; he had never, that was certain, seen all seven at once. It was a shock his wife had spared him.

And this:

Juliet had already seated herself in the driver's seat, her whip set at the correct angle, the reins smartly assembled. She looked quite enchanting.

Indeed she caught the eye of the Governor himself. He was, at that moment, trotting past, helter-skelter, with a great clattering of hooves, as he was driving tandem in his London Curricle.

His Excellency was a descendant of King Charles the Second —as indeed who is not?—and whenever he appeared in Parramatta all women between the ages of sixteen and sixty would inviolably withdraw into hiding until he had passed.

With predatory smiles creasing his distinctly "Caroline", rubicund, yet swarthy face, he was about to pull up beside Juliet when the A.D.C.-in-Waiting leant across to say urgently, "That is Miss Juliet McCree, the grand-daughter of the Vicar of Mallow's Marsh, and she is twelve years old"—and clucked twice (to the horses). "She is a personable girl for her age," commented Sir Charles, as he acknowledged salutes from Dr Phantom and the Vicar and the small crowd that had quickly gathered, and he moved off reluctantly with a spectacular display of horsemanship.

It would be even more ridiculous to try to summarize these stories. The two main characters are, I suppose, Dr Phantom and Dr Boisragon, who are partners in medical practice but in every other way opposed. Dr Phantom is kind, generous, romantic and, until the very end of the book, a bachelor. Dr Boisragon is selfish, complacent, arrogant and very much married (his first wife dies giving birth to her twentieth child; he then promptly marries again). Most of the other characters are related, closely or distantly, to Dr Boisragon. (As an experiment I constructed a family tree which actually worked!) After the two doctors, the principles are the family McCree, the Rector and his wife, their widowed daughter-in-law, the flighty Peronel, and their grand-children, Donalbain and the enchanting Juliet McCree.

A good many of these characters are introduced in the brilliant first chapter which seems to me the very summit of Ethel Anderson's achievement. (Unfortunately none of the others quite reaches this peak.) Dr Phantom returns from a visit to his patients laden with gifts of fruit to discover a children's party in progress at his partner's house. But something is wrong. He is baffled at the sight of "seven little boys and girls, of ages ranging from four to, perhaps, ten or eleven years, each holding in their trembling hands a black papier-mâché basin; each standing on a separate step of the stone stair-way that led down to the slowly-meandering waters of the Lane Cove River."

Dr Boisragon, looking even more stern than usual, informs him that one of the children has stolen an apricot—a Red Roman—which he was keeping for his wife. Since none of them will admit to the theft, he has determined on a scientific experiment. He has given all the children an emetic. The two doctors stand on the step nibbling fruit from an ample basket until nature takes its course.

Juliet McPhee is discovered to be the culprit. Dr Boisragon is outraged by her perfidy, though the child argues that it was not theft because she did not know that the Red Roman belonged to anyone.

> But don't you see, Uncle Peter, it is only you who see anything wrong in it? When Papa used to go shooting duck—whose ducks did he shoot? And when you go catching fish—whose fish do you catch? And you know perfectly well that when God gave Adam the earth—as for all I can learn He did—He gave him every blessed thing! And I have never heard anyone say that what belonged to Adam does not belong to me. And whether I took a Red Roman, or whether any of my cousins, or my brother Donalbain (who is four) took a Red Roman, it is only a person like you, who thinks so much of owning a thing, who makes a sin of it. It is just the natural thing to do.

Juliet is packed off home in disgrace with the First Murderer. The other children (slightly pale) continue their games. Dr Phantom and Dr Boisragon go down to the river.

> "At this time of the evening," Dr Boisragon took Dr Phantom's arm, "it is pleasant to sit on the steps facing the water, where one occasionally gets a puff of sea-air, and since the children's party is in full swing in the house, let us linger here for an hour before going indoors."
>
> The partners took their places on the step where the basket of mixed fruits still adorned the parapet. Dr Phantom, having set down his own basket of pears by his side, made an incision in a Golden Pear of Xaintonge with thirty-two sharp white teeth.
>
> "I have been thinking over that depraved girl's case," Dr Boisragon murmured, having embarked on a second pear. "I see that her first sin—*theft*—was the cause of her second sin—

lying—but, delving more deeply into the cause of her crimes, I am of the considered opinion that the child's inability to control her carnal appetite was the primal reason for her downfall. *That girl is a glutton!* Did you notice the way she kept eyeing these grapes?"

"Yes, I did," Dr Phantom rejoined, averting his eyes.

And there I rest my case. If I have not by now persuaded you that Ethel Anderson's was a rare and delicate talent, and that *At Parramatta* is a minor Australian classic which should be reprinted, re-read and accepted as such, then I have failed in my endeavour. You will have to be satisfied with Ronald Firbank.

ADVANCE
AUSTRALIA SQUARE

I HAVE long admired the writing of Ross Campbell. If his work is little known to most Australian intellectuals, that is simply because few intellectuals read the Sydney *Daily Telegraph*, the *Sunday Telegraph* and the *Australian Women's Weekly* in which his articles appear. One can understand why; but for those whose professional duties oblige them to read these papers, Ross Campbell is a rich reward. Moreover he has published a selection of these pieces in two little books, *Daddy, Are You Married?* and *Mummy, Who Is Your Husband?* and a third volume, *She Can't Play My Bagpipes*, of articles which appeared in the *Bulletin.** There is now no excuse for ignoring one of Australia's best humorous writers. (The best is Barry Oakley by a furlong.)

Daddy, Are You Married? and *Mummy, Who Is Your Husband?* are chiefly devoted to the goings on of the Campbell family in Oxalis Cottage ("a suburban house of 15 squares, including myself") though a few of them deal with topics of general interest like putting out the garbage and the curious fact that dentists never appear as heroes or lovers in television serials. On the whole I prefer the latter. A very little about other people's children goes a long way. *She Can't Play My*

* All these are published by the Shakespeare Head Press.

Bagpipes is a selection of longer and slightly more sophisticated articles—one might almost call them essays if one did not feel that the word might offend the author. All of them are very funny.

Ross Campbell himself is excessively modest. Indeed it is part of his pose—and therefore, perhaps, not altogether sincere —to depict himself always as an average sort of middle-class fellow without any unusual qualities or experience, a bit of a failure in his profession but a good husband and father. In the blurbs to his books he describes himself wittily as "a tame colonial boy" and "a typical soft-bitten Aussie". In one of his essays he admits to having been a "trepid airman" in the Second World War. Usually, however, he is careful to avoid wit, which, perhaps, he considers too closely allied to the kind of intellectual pretentiousness that is his chief dislike. I do not know why this is so. At times he still seems to be reacting against Oxford where he was a Rhodes Scholar and where, one must admit, intellectual pretension and intellectual snobbery are extremely common. But so is wit; and I cannot help regretting that Ross Campbell, who in real life is one of the wittiest of men (he once wrote to me that his only surviving ambitions were to read Latin like a don and drive like a taxi-driver: unfortunately, he said, so far he had managed only to drive like a don and read Latin like a taxi-driver) should have so sternly suppressed this side of his nature in his writing. He allows it to emerge occasionally in his book reviews in the *Daily Telegraph* which I admire even more than his various columns.

His writing is always deceptively simple, both in style and subject matter. I say "deceptively" because, of course, this extreme simplicity conceals considerable art as well as a very shrewd and perceptive view of life. Ross Campbell is not really a simple man though he has chosen to write for simple men and women. In the case of the Oxalis Cottage pieces this simplicity is taken, I feel, to extreme lengths, even though they obviously are written for a mass audience. Few sentences have more than twelve words. No word would present the least difficulty to a third form school boy. Moreover his customary pose of being an average man, an ordinary bloke, sometimes becomes irritating. The only films or television programmes that are mentioned are those that appeal to a mass audience; the only books are best sellers of the most popular kind. In one piece Campbell does admit to be reading *Dr Zhivago*, but manages to imply that he has stuck at page 253.

Yet what delightful comic effects he can achieve within this convention! In fairness to readers who do not know his work well I must quote two fairly substantial extracts. The first, on one of his favourite subjects, is from *Mummy, Who Is Your Husband?*.

According to my calculations I have carried the garbage tin to the front gate 1,563 times.

Correction—1,562 times. Once after a party last year I fell asleep without carrying the tin out.

Aub and Nev, the council collectors, did not come down the path and get it. They are strict men, who believe that if you give a ratepayer an inch he will take a back-yard.

In fifteen years of handling garbage, I have learned a few points of technique.

My packing of the tin has improved. I do not resort so often to the crude method of jumping on the contents.

Also I pack garbage *inside* garbage. If there is an empty spaghetti or jam tin I put bacon rind or rice pudding, say, inside it to save space. This trick has been valuable since the Council's petty refusal to empty more than one garbage tin at a time.

All these 1,562 times I have taken the tin to the gate unassisted. My wife stubbornly refuses to participate. So the whole weight of the family garbage has fallen on me.

Lately I have not felt the same zest for the job. Neighbours have noticed that when I take bundles of fishbones or potato peelings outside I seem listless, lacking in pep. They recognise the symptoms of garbage fatigue.

One night this week I worked late. On the way home I remembered glumly it was garbage night.

To my amazement the tin was outside the gate. I had never seen it happen before.

Going inside, I gasped: "The garbage tin! Who took it out?"

Lancelot was looking modestly proud. "I did," he said.

I thanked him warmly and said: "Pretty heavy, wasn't it?"

"It wasn't so bad. I've been doing weight-lifting at school," he replied.

I gave him some tips on packing garbage in the tin. He seems to have a feeling for it. Yesterday when the tin was full he squeezed in a big bundle of crusts and pea-shells.

When I told my wife how delighted I was by Lancelot's progress, she took it calmly.

She is more excited because Theodora does some of the ironing.

"Did you know Baby Pip can tidy her table?" she said.

Pip gave an exhibition of stacking her plastic sewing machine, tea-set and doll's groceries in a heap.

"I pick up the chesses too," she said, complacently pointing to the chess set.

But it means more to me to have a boy who is able to help with the garbage.

From now on it will not be such a lonely struggle.

The other quotation is one of my favourites. It comes from one of the longer, more sophisticated articles in the *Bulletin* and displays perfectly that wry, gentle, human and self-deprecating humour which is Ross Campbell's speciality. Unfortunately it is too long to quote in full.

The hazards of being tattooed have been demonstrated in a striking way by a sad case in Britain. A young lady there, in a mood of irresponsible euphoria, had the word "Mild" tattooed on one breast and "Bitter" on the other. Her father complained that these inscriptions had since caused her much embarrassment and had seriously reduced her chances of making a suitable and happy marriage.

The tattooing, we must presume, was undertaken originally as a joke. In certain company and certain circumstances, it might conceivably be regarded as not a bad joke. Its appeal is limited and regional, since the selling of ale in the categories Mild and Bitter is a purely British custom. In a wine-drinking country the young lady might have achieved more effect by the labels "Rouge" and "Blanc". In Sydney, where many people are accustomed to the products of Tooth's Brewery, a more appropriate legend would be "Old" and "New". None the less we can imagine that when she first displayed her pectoral captions to a sympathetic English audience she got a laugh.

Her mistake lay in giving the permanence of tattooing to this fleeting jest. Soon, no doubt, the amusement died down. She was branded socially as the Mild and Bitter girl. . . .

The ephemeral nature of humour makes it essentially opposed to the durability of tattooing. That is why anyone who has ever tried to be funny—whether in print, on the stage or TV screen, or simply on social occasions—must feel an instinctive sympathy for the Mild and Bitter girl. She has been punished for forgetting that the world does not laugh at the same joke twice.

The life of the party can offer to abandon an anecdote if his audience has heard it before. But it is hopeless for the Mild and Bitter girl to say: "Stop me if you've seen this one." She is, as modern thinkers say, committed to her single built-in sight-gag. . . .

Yet I feel that the future is not necessarily as bleak as she and her father believe. The fickle public may have deserted her in favour of entertainers with more novel quips. But she will find warmth and compassion among those who know by experience the risks and difficulties of the droll. Some humorous columnist, or cartoonist, or comedy scriptwriter will offer tenderness to the Mild and Bitter girl, will make her his bosom friend and perhaps his bride.

He will understand. He will not blame her for having a chestnut that she can never get off her chest.

It is worth while studying these two passages in detail. Both are written in clear, correct and classical prose. It is easy and colloquial but not slangy. There is no hint of journalese, and clichés are rigorously excluded. (Clichés are one of Ross Campbell's favourite targets, and some of his best pieces make fun of them.) In the second article he has allowed himself a richer vocabulary and reveals an admirable choice of words. The words on the young lady's chest are correctly described as "inscriptions", "labels", "legend" and "pectoral captions". There is never a sentence that causes the reader the slightest difficulty in immediately perceiving the author's meaning. These are not easy accomplishments, as the prose style of so many of our politicians and academics reveals. If I wished to refer a young cadet reporter to a model for a good plain style for use in newspapers, I might suggest to him Hazlitt or Bernard Shaw or David Hume or Bertrand Russell if I thought he might read these authors, but I should feel perfectly happy to recommend Ross Campbell.

Campbell has also mastered perfectly the technique, so

necessary for a journalist or a humorist, of making his first paragraph both amusing in itself and an irresistable lure for what follows. A favourite device is to take some familiar proposition and turn it neatly on its head. Here is an excellent example:

> "The children have been reading more lately," my wife said. "It's interfering with their television."
> "There's no harm in that," I said. "Some of the stuff in books is very educational."

Or this:

> The problems of mistresses are being given a hearing at last. In a TV program called "The Other Woman" the BBC interviewed a representative group of concubines, and viewers were shocked by the unhappiness and hardships that were laid bare. The women were grossly neglected by their lovers, who often spent most of the time with their wives. It was made plain that mistresses had no security of tenure, no prospect of promotion, and no superannuation rights.

In a slightly different vein I like this opening: "I had some drinks last week with the Vert brothers—Intro, Extra, Con, and Per. They are an interesting family, widely divergent in their tastes, yet retaining something in common." Like many writers Ross Campbell is fascinated by words, their use, misuse and abuse (the habit is catching). He is especially good on Lost Positives, like scrutable, trepid, and peccable. He is less happy with puns, of which he is fond, but occasionally he has a beauty. My favourite occurs in this passage: "I noticed she was slapping her legs. I got the spray to check the mossies. A few squirts sent them growling into a corner, but they came back fighting. They are dinkum mossies." He is also an excellent parodist when he chooses, though parody is generally avoided as hinting, if only slightly, of intellectual superiority —after all one must have *read* an author in order to appreciate a parody—unless he is simply parodying an ad man or a television announcer. He shows what he can do, however, in that excellent essay "Captain Cook takes a Captain Cook" where eighteenth century diction is beautifully taken off. (Ross Campbell read English literature under C. S. Lewis at Oxford!)

But all these things, verbal dexterity, puns, jokes, an ability to parody, even an admirable prose style, are merely the tools of a humorist's trade. If he is to be taken seriously he must also have something to say about life, some point of view or criticism to make, some message to communicate beyond mere entertainment. And here Ross Campbell leaves me uneasy. For it seems to me that he manages to express at the same time—perhaps unconsciously—some of the best Australian qualities and some of the worst.

Let us take the best first. Ross Campbell is a democrat by instinct as most Australians are, but he has added to this basic democracy a slightly novel twist. Few people now claim that some men are better than others because they were born in a higher class or went to a better school. That kind of snobbery is out of date. But there is a very strong tendency to replace this old class distinction by a belief that people can be graded by their tastes. On this theory, for instance, wine drinkers are better than beer drinkers, those whose homes are decorated in a Japanese or Finnish style better than those who have gnomes in the garden and ducks on the wall, and those who enjoy conceptual art are infinitely superior to those who like paintings of gum-trees. Ross Campbell rejects this heresy absolutely. He enjoys making fun of the wine and food snobs and makes it plain that he is on the side of those who put a bottle of Heinz tomato sauce on the table. He is equally severe on the cult of the beautiful people.

> It is part of the new doctrine that things are better if they are associated with beautiful people. A pernicious example is the publishing of recipes recommended by lovely actresses. These dishes are nearly always unpalatable. I put my trust in plain cooks and plain authors.
>
> The publishing house of Collins has sent me an impressive photograph of Winston Graham, author of the novel *The Walking Stick*. Half-bald, he has bags under his eyes like a basset hound, crow's feet, and an air of total disenchantment. I look forward to reading Mr Graham's novel. He looks as if he could write.

I find this healthy scepticism about the fashionable, the modish and the new congenial. I like to think that it is, in fact, an Australian characteristic which may save this nation from some of the more lunatic follies that prevail in Britain and the United States. Ross Campbell simply does not believe a woman writer who tells him that childbirth is really rather a jolly experience. He is sceptical of those who extol the advantages of permissive sex. He suspects that priests who rush into marriage may soon be regretting celibacy. The guff and gush of ad. men, press relations, TV communicators leave him cold and disbelieving. He is quite content to be unfashionable, non-swinging and square.

Of course a humorist who sets out to make fun of pretension runs certain risks. It is fatally easy to mock things that are in fact good just because they are unfamiliar. Here, I think, Ross Campbell is extremely shrewd. He is careful to avoid subjects like art which, however tempting to the satirist, are perilous for those who know nothing about it. He tackles intellectual and artistic subjects only where he feels sure of his ground, as with books and literature. On these Ross Campbell's judgement seems to me to be generally sound though I do not always agree with him. (For instance I cannot understand why he finds Furphy's *Such is Life* an overrated bore: it is an undisciplined book, but some passages in it are almost as funny as, say, Ross Campbell.) But certainly no other critic in Australia is so skilled in picking out and dissecting a bad pretentious book.

No, my real quarrel with Ross Campbell is different. It is that he deliberately reinforces the common Australian suspicion of all intellectual effort as high-faluting, pretentious and therefore un-Australian. It is one thing to say that a man who likes Boulez or Stockhausen is not *morally* superior to a man who likes Gilbert and Sullivan, or that a man who reads Proust is not *morally* superior to a man who prefers the adventures of James Bond. But it is wrong to suggest that he is not intellectually superior and downright dangerous to suggest that he is morally *inferior*. I feel that Ross Campbell gets very close to this proposition at times, particularly in his Oxalis Cottage pieces. There is a subtle suggestion that the ordinary suburban man is as good as, if not better than, anyone else and that intellectual effort is unnecessary for the good life.

In fairness, I think Ross Campbell himself feels uneasy about this. Occasionally he manages to put in a suggestion that reading, for instance, is a normal and healthy occupation! In his *Bulletin* pieces and book reviews he may even reveal himself as the scholar he is. But for the most part he scrupulously avoids the least suspicion of scholarship or knowledge or intelligence. One is left with the strong impression that after supper at Oxalis Cottage—or should I say "tea"— Mr and Mrs Campbell, Theodora, Lancelot, Little Nell and Baby Pip gather round and sing those verses by Henry Lawson which should, I sometimes think, be the Australian national anthem:

But the curse of class distinctions from our shoulders shall be
    hurled;
An' the sense of Human Kinship revolutionise the world;
There'll be higher education for the toilin', starvin' clown,
An' the rich and educated shall be educated down!

And somehow I don't believe they do!

LITERARY MIGRANTS

SOME of the most famous English migrants to sail for Australia never arrived. They are the select band of literary migrants whose authors, throughout the nineteenth century, dispatched them to the colonies whenever they had become inconvenient and required a quick but merciful end. Long after the convict system had been brought to an end, British novelists and poets continued to sentence their creatures to transportation for the term of their unnatural lives. If literary migrants could be added to real ones, Australia should be in a fair way to over-population.

Generally, but not always, there is some excuse for this conduct. The characters chosen for this fate have either failed in England or have disgraced themselves in some way. It is assumed by their authors that they will get a second chance in Australia and, if they fail again or continue their career of crime, then Australians will be less likely to complain. Sometimes it is hinted, not too delicately, that since all Australians are convicts, a few more will hardly be noticed. The authors rarely stop to consider whether these characters themselves would be happier in their new country.

There are many amusing examples of this summary justice. Typical, perhaps, is that unfortunate Mr Gigadibs who is suddenly dispatched by Robert Browning in the last ten lines of "Bishop Blougram". "Bishop Blougram" is a magnificent poem for which I have the greatest admiration, but poor Gigadibs never has a chance. This brash young man— a journalist of sorts—after being annihilated by the Bishop in a long argument during which he never, in fact, utters a word, is packed off to Australia at short notice.

> He did not sit five minutes. Just a week
> Sufficed his sudden healthy vehemence.
> (Something had struck him in the 'Outward Bound'
> Another way than Blougram's purpose was)
> And having bought, not cabin-furniture
> But settler's implements (enough for three)
> And started for Australia—there, I hope,
> By this time he has tested his first plough,
> And studied his last chapter of St John.

No, it won't do. With the best will in the world I cannot see Gigadibs as a cocky farmer on the Western slopes. He gave it away after a few months; sold his plough; tried the goldfields; and ended, a hopeless drunk, as a poorly paid subeditor on a Church newspaper!

In his delightful *New Arabian Nights* Robert Louis Stevenson, who, as noted earlier, later visited Australia himself, dispatched *two* of his minor characters in this way. In the affair of "The Rajah's Diamond" the charming but effeminate Harry Hartley, who is meant to be Sir Thomas Vandeleur's private secretary but spends his time running errands for his beautiful wife, becomes innocently involved in the theft of the diamond. He is dismissed from Sir Thomas's service and threatened with arrest, "but to the unfortunate secretary the whole affair was the beginning of a new and manlier life. The police were convinced of his innocence; and, after he had given what help he could in the subsequent investigations, he was even complimented by one of the chiefs of the detective department on the probity and simplicity of his behaviour. Several persons interested themselves in one so unfortunate; and soon after he inherited a sum of money from a maiden aunt in Worcestershire. With this he married Prudence, and set sail for Bendigo, or according to another account, for Trincomalee, exceedingly content, and with the best of prospects." Since Harry is earlier described as "blond and pink, with dove's eyes and a gentle smile . . . and the most submissive and caressing manners", I rather hope it was Trincomalee. I do not think that Bendigo was Harry's scene.

Not content with this, Stevenson, only a few pages later, dispatches yet another character to Australia. This time it is the clergyman Rolles who has been corrupted by the lure of the Rajah's diamond and finally confesses his part to the magnificent Prince Florizel, Prince of Bohemia.

> They spoke much together, and the clergyman was more than once affected to tears by the mingled severity and tenderness of Florizel's reproaches.
>
> "I have made ruin of my life," he said at last. "Help me; tell me what I am to do; I have, alas! neither the virtues of a priest nor the dexterity of a rogue."
>
> "Now that you are humbled," said the Prince, "I command no longer; the repentant have to do with God, and not with Princes. But if you will let me advise you, go to Australia as a colonist, seek menial labour in the open air, and try to forget that you have ever been a clergyman, or that you ever set eyes on that accursed stone.

To deal with two characters in this way in the same tale seems a trifle careless. However, Stevenson made amends when he eventually came to Sydney and created the remittance man, Carthew, in *The Wrecker*, who is actually sent home again!

A still more unlikely settler is Algernon in Oscar Wilde's *The Importance of Being Ernest*. Fortunately Algernon is saved, but only after Cecily has frightened him out of his wits—his only real asset—by telling him that Uncle Jack wants to speak to him about his emigrating:

CECILY: But still I think you had better wait until Uncle Jack arrives. I know he wants to speak to you about your emigrating.

ALGERNON: About my what?

CECILY: Your emigrating. He has gone out to buy your outfit.

ALGERNON: I certainly wouldn't let Jack buy my outfit. He has no taste in neckties at all.

CECILY: I don't think you will require neckties. Uncle Jack
            is sending you to Australia.
ALGERNON: Australia! I'd sooner die.
CECILY: Well, he said at dinner on Wednesday night, that
            you would have to choose between this world, the
            next world and Australia.
ALGERNON: Oh, well! The accounts I have received of Australia
            and the next world are not particularly encouraging.
            This world is good enough for me, cousin Cecily.

It is, perhaps, amusing to consider what Algernon would
have done if he had been sent to Australia. My own view is
that, after losing all his money on some absurd scheme like
selling spats to boundary riders, he would have been appointed an attaché to a Governor—probably to that Lord Lundy
who is himself one of the most illustrious of all literary
migrants in Hilaire Belloc's *Cautionary Tales*:

> The Duke—his aged grandsire—bore
> The shame till he could bear no more.
> He rallied his declining powers
> Summoned the youth to Brackley Towers,
> And bitterly addressed him thus—
> 'Sir! you have disappointed us!
> We had intended you to be
> The next Prime Minister but three:
> The stocks were sold; the press was squared:
> The middle-class was quite prepared.
> But as it is! . . . my language fails!
> Go out and govern New South Wales!'

There are, however, two more serious attempts to use
emigration to Australia as a theme in nineteenth century
novels. In *David Copperfield* Charles Dickens sends out a
whole shipload of his characters. Even if we do not count
David and Dora's "page" who is transported (literally) for
theft quite early in the story, Mr and Mrs Micawber, their
five—or is it six?—children, old Mr Peggotty, Mrs Gummidge,
Little Em'ly and the unfortunate Martha are all dispatched
in this way towards the end of the book. There is admittedly
something absurd about this wholesale emigration. Many
critics have pointed out that the feckless though charming

Mr Micawber hardly seems suitable material to make a good settler. Also the only reason given for Mr Peggotty taking Little Em'ly to Australia—that she may live down the shame of her seduction by Steerforth—is inadequate even if one accepts the Victorian view of her offence. It would surely have been enough for her to move to another town in England where no one knew her. The same thing applies to Martha, "the fallen woman", who (though Dickens never tells us this in so many words) has become a prostitute, though it is typical of Mr Peggotty's goodness that he should take the girl with him.

Because of these flaws some critics have suggested that emigration is simply a device to get rid of these characters at the end of the book. But this is unfair. Arthur Calder-Marshall has pointed out that Dickens who, in his own life, worked both for the rescue of "fallen women" and the assistance of emigrants to Australia,* had a strong belief that, given a second chance, people who had once failed might make good. Indeed the Second Chance is one of the main themes of *David Copperfield*.

In the very first chapter Betsey Trotwood, who has lost the chance of a child of her own, is given a first chance, as an aunt, of welcoming David. She rejects it because his sex is wrong. When David turns up at Dover, she seizes her second chance, and gives David *his* second chance of an education (such as Dickens himself had). Mr Dick, having been written off as an amiable loon, is given his second chance, when Betsey loses her money, by learning to copy legal documents. Mr Wickfield, brought to ruin by his alcoholic cultivation of the memory of his dead wife, gets his second chance when he realises his mistake.

In Dickens's mind, therefore, emigration to Australia is a second chance for Little Em'ly, for Martha and even for the Micawbers, though, of course, he does not miss the chance to exploit the comic elements in this situation. When David's aunt informs the Micawbers that she has arranged for their emigration to Australia, they accept the news bravely.

* Two of Dickens's own children later emigrated to Australia.

"There is but one question, my dear ma'am, I could wish to ask," said Mrs Micawber. "The climate, I believe, is healthy?" "Finest in the world," said my aunt. "Just so," returned Mrs Micawber.

"Then my question arises. Now, are the circumstances of the country such, that a man of Mr Micawber's abilities would have a fair chance of rising in the social scale? I will not say, at present, might he aspire to be governor, or anything of that sort; but would there be a reasonable opening for his talents to develop themselves—that would be amply sufficient—and find their own expansion?"

"No better opening anywhere," said my aunt, "for a man who conducts himself well, and is industrious."

"For a man who conducts himself well," repeated Mrs Micawber, with her clearest business manner, "and is industrious. Precisely. It is evident to me that Australia is the legitimate sphere of action for Mr Micawber."

"I entertain the conviction, my dear madam," said Mr Micawber, "that it is, under existing circumstances, the land, the only land, for myself and family; and that something of an extraordinary nature will turn up on that shore."

Moreover Dickens, unlike most of the other authors who used this device, does not desert his characters entirely. As if aware of the reader's slight unease about the fate of the Micawbers in their new country, he deliberately brings Mr Peggotty back on a visit to England in the second last chapter to tell us how the emigrants fared. They have fared well. After working hard in the bush on a little farm, Mr Peggotty, Mrs Gummidge and Little Em'ly have prospered and retired to the town of Port Middlebay Harbour." (Has anyone tried to guess where this was?) Martha has married a farm labourer, and they live "fower hundred mile away from any voices but their own and the singing birds". Little Em'ly, of course, would not marry, though she had plenty of opportunity, because this is Dickens and the Victorian novel. Mrs Gummidge has also refused an offer! As for the Micawbers, they have flourished. After working in the bush Mr Micawber has become a magistrate at Port Middlebay and a leading citizen of the town.

And, after all, is this so absurd? Australia is a country where "something of an extraordinary nature"—like iron ore and nickel and uranium—does often turn up when it is most needed. Mr Micawber himself, feckless, tipsy, improvident as he is, has a certain bounce and exuberance which are not un-Australian characteristics. Certainly I like to think that Mr Micawber took his second chance.

Dickens was the first to use emigration to Australia in a novel. *David Copperfield* appeared in serial form in 1849. The last book I propose to deal with—though far from the last in which the theme appears—was published at the very end of the nineteenth century. It is *Jude The Obscure*. In it Hardy does something quite new. He sends one of his characters to Australia not to get rid of her finally but to keep her out of the way for a time. He then brings her back again, changed and hardened by the experience but in a natural and convincing way. One feels that at last going to Australia has been accepted, not as the end of everything, not even as the beginning of a new and different life, but as something which can happen to anyone. Arabella Fawley is not "sent" to Australia; she goes of her own free will and returns of her own free will.

Arabella is the handsome country girl who attracts Jude's attention by throwing a pig's pizzle at him—one of the most daring scenes in Victorian fiction. She is "a complete and substantial female animal—no more, no less" and she sets out to capture Jude merely to prove her sexual power, for the scholarly young man with ambitions to rise in the Church is quite unsuited to her. She deliberately seduces him and then pretends that she is pregnant, confident that so honest a young man will marry her. He does—and the result, of course, is disastrous. They have nothing in common. Jude learns he has been tricked into marriage. Arabella is disappointed in her catch. One night he goes home to find her gone and a note saying that she is going to Australia with her parents. "A woman of her sort would have more chance over there than in this stupid country."

Jude goes to Christminster (Oxford) to pursue his interrupted studies. He meets and falls in love with another girl, his cousin, Sue Bridehead, but she marries another, older, man. Time passes but Jude remains a poor working man, barred from the education he craves by the barriers of class

prejudice. One night he enters an inn for a drink and finds
that Arabella is one of the barmaids. She is joking with a
customer about the "husband" she left in Australia.

Jude speaks to her and finds she has returned from Sydney
about three months before. "He observed that her hands
were smaller and whiter than when he had lived with her,
and that on the hand which pulled the beer-engine she wore
an ornamental ring set with what seemed to be real sapphires
—which they were indeed, and were much admired as such
by the young men who frequented the bar." She persuades
him to take her to a neighbouring town where Jude has to
go, in order to "talk things over". They stay the night at the
local inn and once again Arabella's sexual magnetism pre-
vails. They sleep together. After all, Jude thinks, they are
man and wife. On the way home Arabella reveals to him that
while in Australia she had "married" the manager of a Sydney hotel and lived with him "honourably enough, and as
respectable as any married couple in the Colony". She has
in fact committed bigamy. Jude is appalled and once again
feels that he has been tricked.

The rest of the novel concerns the curious relations between Jude, Arabella and Sue. Arabella is a coarse, immoral,
selfish woman; Sue is sensitive, good and devoted. But Arabella remains to the end, when she leaves Jude dead in his
bed to go down to watch the boat races on the river, the
more real and living of the two women. And she is the only
one of all the literary migrants whom I can recognize in
Australia. I see her in the old Aaron's Hotel in Sydney near
closing time, leaning over the bar to joke with the customers
and show off her full figure, as she appeared to Jude in the
inn at Christminster: "The faces of the barmaidens had
risen in colour, each having a pink flush on her cheek; their
manners were still more vivacious than before—more abandoned, more excited, more sensuous, and they expressed their
sentiments and desires less euphemistically, laughing in a
lackadaisical tone, without reserve." How naturally she
would fit that scene! And Arabella might surely have found
happiness in Australia if her destiny had not been to go
back to England to drag Jude down with her to the mire
from which he had struggled in vain to rise.

A DEATH
ON THE CLARENCE

O N the afternoon of Tuesday, 30th April 1968, a farmer called John Chapman, who had a small property at Southampton on the Clarence in New South Wales, was rowing his boat to Grafton with two of his children. (At that time boats were the normal means of travel in the Grafton district since there were virtually no roads and very few could afford a horse.) One of the children noticed an object floating in the river and said, "Father, look, what is that?" John Chapman replied that it might possibly be a dead body but it was too far away to tell. On his way home, however, between 4 and 5 p.m., he kept his boat in the stream where the floating thing was most likely to be, and soon found it about a mile upstream from where he had first seen it. It had been carried there by the wind and tide. With the help of two men in another boat, Chapman lifted the body out of the water—for it was a dead man—and the other two men took the sodden corpse back to Grafton. Chapman noticed that "one eye was staring and open; the other closed as in sleep; the eye open appeared to be injured; his dress was in no way disturbed."

This was the end of one of the most melancholy and mysterious stories in Australian literary history. The body was that of James Lionel Michael, a solicitor of Grafton, who had disappeared from his home two days before, on the evening of Sunday, 28th April. Michael is best known as the man who befriended the poet Henry Kendall, but he was also a minor poet in his own right, and his story is such a curious one and so little known that it is worth retelling today.*

James Lionel Michael was born in Red Lion Square in London in 1824. His father was a well-to-do solicitor; his mother, the sister of a well-known wine merchant. Michael was the eldest of six or seven children all of whom received a good education. On leaving school Michael was articled to his father and eventually qualified as a solicitor though he disliked the law. His own tastes were literary and artistic, and he soon began writing verse. He also became interested in the work of those painters who called themselves the Pre-Raphaelite Brotherhood and wrote a pamphlet defending their aims against criticism. Through this he got to know Ruskin and Millais who thought he might make an excellent art-critic. He began to make a name for himself in artistic and literary circles in London.

In 1853, however, when twenty-nine years of age, he decided to emigrate to Australia. Just why he did this is not known. In one of his poems, "Retrospection", written in 1861, he says that it was because of a disappointed love affair. His Sydney friend Sheridan Moore, the poetic teacher, said that it was because of financial difficulties. Perhaps this is more likely. Gold had just been discovered in Australia, and many young Englishmen, some of them wildly unsuitable, were setting off to seek their fortune on the diggings. The Pre-Raphaelites, oddly enough, seem to have been peculiarly vulnerable to gold-fever. Another young poet and sculptor, Thomas Woolner, one of the seven original members of the Brotherhood, sailed for Australia in July 1852, with two other artists, Edward Latrobe Batman and Bernhard Smith. Holman Hunt, the two Rossettis and Ford Madox Brown went down to Gravesend to see them off, and

---

* For the sake of those scholars who may be interested, this account is based chiefly on J. Sheridan Moore's *Life and Genius of James Lionel Michael*, James Tyrrell's *Postscript* to his *Old Books, Old Friends, Old Sydney*, which includes the previously unpublished poems of Michael; and the report of the inquest on Michael from the *Sydney Morning Herald* of 11th May 1868, which is also included in Tyrrell's *Postscript*.

it was this scene which inspired Ford Madox Brown's famous painting, "The Last of England".

Unlike Woolner, Michael never went to the gold-fields and never returned to England. On his arrival in Sydney in 1853 he very sensibly decided that not only was he quite unsuited to the rough life of the diggings but that his chances of finding gold were extremely remote. Instead, he set up as a practising solicitor in Sydney and resumed his true profession of writing poetry in his leisure hours.

It was not long before Michael met other literary men in Sydney. The first occasion—like nearly everything else in Michael's story—was a curious one. One day in 1853 Sheridan Moore was trying to catch a train at Newtown station. "In springing into a railway carriage while the train was in motion"—I am quoting Moore's own account—"some portion of my dress caught in the door, and only for the timely assistance of the guard, I should probably have fallen back and been killed, or much hurt. During the flurry this occasioned, a middle-aged women asked, with kindly severity, 'Do you want to kill yourself?' 'No, madam,' I answered, perhaps too flippantly, 'I do not wish to discover the Great Secret in that rough way.'

" 'Particularly,' said a lively gentleman opposite, 'as a drop of concentrated Prussic acid would do that for you much neater.' 'Thanks for the information,' I replied; 'but we don't destroy what we like, or you would not take such care of those flowers'—for the gentleman had an elegant bouquet in his hand."

The "lively gentleman" was James Lionel Michael and by the time the train had reached Central Station they had struck up an acquaintance.

I have quoted this absurd story in full, partly because of its rich Victorian character; partly because it gives us the only vivid glimpse of Michael himself; but partly because it contains two possible clues to the mysteries of Michael's life and death. Since I am not writing a detective story I will mention them now. Firstly, Michael's odd remark reveals his interest both in chemistry and suicide. (In fact he was an amateur chemist of some ability.) Secondly, the bouquet suggests that he was going to visit a lady. Men do not usually carry flowers for any other reason—at least not in the train from Newtown to Central Station.

Sheridan Moore introduced Michael to his circle of literary friends including Stenhouse, Deniehy, Silvester and others whose names mean little to us now. More important, he introduced him to the poet Henry Kendall "whom he received as an affectionate elder brother would a younger one from whom he had long been separated". The facts about Kendall's life have been told many times. They are almost unbearably painful. His English father and Irish mother, though kindly and talented, were both feckless and drunken. Kendall's boyhood was one of fearful hardship and poverty. When Michael first met him he was still only eighteen or nineteen, not long returned from his voyage to the South Seas as a cabin-boy on a whaling ship.

Michael was the first really well-educated man Kendall had met. He was a Latin scholar, spoke French and Italian and understood German and Spanish. Moreover he had a library. He introduced Kendall to the works of Wordsworth, Shelley, Elizabeth Barret Browning and Swinburne—not all of whom were a good influence on the young man with his fatal facility for easy words and easy sentiment. He also helped him to learn French in order to read Hugo and Béranger. He encouraged him to persevere with his own poetry. Most important of all, perhaps, he gave him a job as a clerk in his office in Sydney in order to relieve him from the drudgery of earning his living—and keeping a home for his mother, brother and sisters—by working as an errand boy for Biddell Brothers at Brickfield Hill and as assistant to a draper in Pitt Street. It is hard to exaggerate his kindness and generosity.

The relationship might have been perfect if Michael had not himself been a poet. During his stay in Sydney Michael published two volumes of verse: *Songs without Music* (1857) and a long autobiographical poem, *John Cumberland* (1860). I do not propose to quote either of them. They have rightly been dismissed by all critics as minor verse, "light, smooth, plaintive and sometimes sweet", which are of no real importance to Australian literature. (Few of the critics, however, seem to have read his later poems, unpublished in his lifetime, which I shall mention later.) But inevitably the older man tended to patronize the younger; while the younger man, aware of his greater talent, resented his advice and criticism.

There was, however, no rift in their friendship when Michael moved to Grafton in 1861. Once again we do not really know why. Was it because he had failed to establish himself as a successful solicitor in Sydney or was it that this time, as I shall suggest later, it really was the consequence of some love affair? For the moment it is sufficient to say that as soon as he had settled in Grafton he sent for Kendall, who became a clerk in his office there in 1862.

There was, in fact, some sense in moving from Sydney to Grafton in 1861. Grafton was then enjoying its first—perhaps its only—"boom" in history. Although it had been proclaimed a municipality only two years before, on 20th July 1859, it was growing rapidly. Gold had been discovered at Solferino in 1856. Crown land along the Clarence was surveyed and sold to settlers from the Hawkesbury and Hunter in 1857. German settlers arrived to set up a factory in the same year. During the same period a steady stream of Highland immigrants from Scotland were arriving in the district, brought out by the Reverend Dunmore Lang to escape the consequences of the harsh Highland Clearances and also (so Mr Lang hoped) to maintain the balance of Presbyterians against the Catholic Irish. In the little township German, Gaelic and even Aboriginal were as likely to be heard as English. There was a sense of excitement in the air, and there were some who were certain that Grafton, with its magnificent site on the Big River, must become the capital of a new State or at least the most important city in northern New South Wales.

Yet it is also important for our story to realize that, for all the bustle and building, Grafton in 1861 was still essentially a primitive bush settlement. There were not more than 1200 souls living in the town itself. Though Mr Surveyor Darke had laid out those superb avenues, those rural Champs Elysées, which so astound the visitor today, in 1848, they were still marked by pegs in the ground or at most by fences. Victoria Street along the river had taken shape but much of Prince Street, the main shopping street today, was still natural forest. The lovely jacarandas and camphor laurels which today provide shade for Grafton's citizens in the heat of summer did not exist. In 1861 men were more concerned with cutting down trees than with planting them.

It was a strange setting for two sensitive and scholarly poets. Yet at first Michael and his poet-clerk seem to have settled down well enough. Michael took a house for himself in the new Victoria Street by the river and an office in Bacon Street. There must have been plenty of work—he was only the second solicitor to arrive in the town—with all that buying and selling of land, and if Michael himself was a rather reluctant lawyer and his clerk almost totally incompetent, would it really have mattered all that much? (I once had occasion to visit a solicitor's office in Grafton and found a handsome cat asleep in the in-tray on top of the filing cabinet. Country style!) Though a man who had known the great world of London and enjoyed the conversation of Ruskin and Millais must have found the society of Grafton in 1861 somewhat limited, Michael was not without friends in the district. He made the acquaintance of a Mr Wilcox, a keen naturalist, of Judge Francis and of Mr Stevenson, the proprietor of the Grafton *Examiner* which had started in 1859. Stevenson became his closest friend.

And then there was the country. Grafton then, as now, must have been a delight to anyone with a taste for natural beauty. There is a magnificence about the Clarence valley which is unrivalled in Australia. The splendid panorama of the New England mountains, the lush, wide water meadows, the great river itself rolling gently down to the sea forty miles away like a minor Mississippi—everything is on a grand and opulent scale. Trees grow into giants in that rich soil. Elsewhere in Australia wattle grows in clumps or is scattered through the bush; in the Clarence valley there are whole forests of lemon-coloured, vanilla-scented trees. The sweet smells hang heavily in that tropical air and there seems to be water everywhere, dripping over the rims of black granite in the mountains, bursting through the foothills in torrents and waterfalls or spreading gently over the flood plain in an intricate maze of islands and marshes.

Both men must have revelled in that beauty. Kendall certainly did. Some of his best poems were written about the Clarence district which he had first known as a boy herding sheep for his father. "Orara", which begins with the well-known lines:

> The strong sob of the chafing stream
> That seaward fights its way
> Down crags of glitter, dells of gleam,
> Is in the hills today.

is written about a tributary of the Clarence which rises on the Dorrigo plateau. (It is worth recalling, however, that while today we can drive up the marvellous roads which rise up from the Bellinger and Clarence valleys through the steep rain forests to the mountains above in a few hours, this rugged country was then inaccessible to all except experienced bushmen. Young Kendall could only look longingly towards the mountains and dream of a beauty he had never seen.)

Michael too must have enjoyed the countryside and, as a keen naturalist, must surely have appreciated the rich animal and bird life of the district. I like to think that Mr Wilcox showed him the haunts of the forest kingfisher and pointed out to him the red-backed kite beating heavily over the river and the giant jabiru stork standing sentinel in the marsh grass—two birds which, to an ornithologist, manage to give to Grafton a distinctly indolent and oriental air.

We do not know exactly when the dream began to fade. The first blow was Kendall's decision to leave. After less than a year the young poet, restless, touchy and dissatisfied, left for Sydney to begin that long slide down to poverty, disease, alcoholism and despair which led to the "Shadow of 1872" when his mind temporarily broke down and he was placed by friends in Gladesville Asylum. There was never an open breach with Michael. He returned to Grafton once more in Michael's lifetime and always remained grateful to the older man's kindness, but his departure must have been a blow to the solitary solicitor.

Michael's business as a solicitor too seems to have declined

and we know from his clerk's evidence—Kendall's successor—
at the inquest that he was "in pecuniary difficulties" when he
died, though how severe these difficulties were it is impossible
to say. He also suffered from bad health though according to
his doctor there was nothing seriously wrong with him. But
he continued to find consolation in his books, his scientific
experiments—he had a "microscopic room" which no one was
permitted to enter—and in writing poetry though he was perfectly aware of his limited talent.

It is at this point I must mention Michael's last poems,
which very few people seem to have read. During his years at
Grafton Michael wrote a number of poems and verse transla-
tions from Béranger. To these he added a few poems written
in Sydney just before he went to Grafton. Michael apparently
contemplated publishing these poems—thirty-six in all—in a
new volume to be called *Miscellaneous Verses*, and during
Kendall's second stay in Grafton he asked the young poet to
copy out these poems for him in his neat and meticulous
script. For some reason these poems were never published in
Michael's lifetime and were not discovered until nearly a
century later when the manuscript (in Kendall's hand and
with dedicatory verses by Kendall) came into the hands of
James Tyrrell, the Sydney bookseller. Tyrrell then published
them as an addendum to his own *Postscript* which had a
limited edition of 500 copies. For all these reasons they have
remained almost unknown to this day.

I would not pretend that these last poems of Michael's are
great poetry. They are simpler, less artificial, than his other
poetry but they must still be considered "minor verse". But
—and this is the point—they contain three or four poems
which unmistakably reveal a mind in torment. These poems
—"The Secret", written as early as 1857, "Retrospection",
written in 1861, and "Introspection" written in 1863—all
have the same theme. The poet complains that he is forced
to wear a mask of calm and indifference to conceal his
anguish, that he moves among friends and acquaintances who
cannot guess the terrible feelings of guilt and remorse which
are destroying him. Here are a few verses of "The Secret",
which seems to me to be the best and most revealing.

We pass our lives behind a mask
    Which no one cares to lift aside,
To see the features right, or ask
    The secret of the man they hide:
Enough if we perform our task
    Decently veil'd—who cares beside;
Though there sleep with us in the urn,
    The ashes of all fires that burn?

What though I hide within my heart,
    The source, not dried, of early tears,
And still in secret feel the smart
    Of wounds that have been scarr'd for years?
That pain I bear, alone, apart,
    And never breathe in others' ears;
No, let the world know all the rest,
    That grief I bury in my breast.

I cry for less and slighter grief,
    Cry out, that all the world may know;
Complain and wail and seek relief
    Of every petty, recent blow,
But this, the saddest and the chief,
    No eye may look upon it—no;
All else the world may see, the whole,
    That is the secret of my soul.

What *was* the secret of James Lionel Michael's soul? We shall never know, but it is perhaps worth discussing—if only to dismiss them—one or two possibilities. One of the poems states clearly that it was not a criminal offence so that we can rule out any conjecture that our solicitor had, perhaps, misappropriated one of his client's funds. Most of them seem to suggest something to do with a love affair which happened either long before in England or at least in his early years in Sydney, but these hints are so vague that they do not carry us much further. Today it is fashionable to see homosexuality in the most unlikely places and I suppose that we should not entirely rule out the possibility that Michael was a secret homosexual and that his friendship for the handsome young boy Kendall was not entirely literary. I certainly cannot disprove this supposition though it seems to me unlikely. Kendall was certainly not a homosexual and there is at least some evidence that Michael was not either.

This brings us straight to the mystery of Michael's private life. We know Michael had a son and that this son was "a native born Australian"—that is to say he was born between the year 1853, when Michael arrived in Australia, and 1868, when he died. But was Michael married? And if so, who was his wife? He was certainly not married when he came to Australia and equally certainly, his wife, if he ever had one, was not living with him in Grafton when he died. There is absolutely no reference to a widow in the evidence given at the inquest. Shortly after his death Sheridan Moore delivered a "discourse" on "The Life and Genius" of his friend at the School of Arts in Sydney on 16th July, 1868. This discourse, which was later published in a limited edition, is an extraordinary production, filled with almost intolerable Victorian sentiment and verbosity, but valuable for the few facts it gives about Michael. It is almost equally valuable for its omissions. Moore, who was Michael's closest friend in Sydney and frequently went to his house in Burwood, mentions his father and mother, his brothers and sisters and even his little boy— but not his wife. There is no mention of her whatever.

Indeed the only mention of a wife which I can find is in one of Michael's strange last poems in which he describes lying awake, in anguish, beside his sleeping "wife" who, like everyone else, does not know the guilt and torment from which he is suffering. This may, of course, have been a purely imaginative flourish or it may have concealed another relationship. The only possible conclusion, I think, is either that Michael was unmarried and that his son was illegitimate— the result of some affair in Sydney, perhaps with the girl to whom he was taking the bouquet of flowers—or that he did marry in Sydney, that his marriage proved disastrous and that his wife left him almost immediately. If his wife had died, Sheridan Moore would surely have mentioned this in his apologia and his grief would surely have been referred to at the inquest. On the whole I think that the evidence points to the conclusion that Michael was unmarried and that his son was illegitimate. Whether this was also the guilty "secret" of his soul it is impossible to say but the existence of an illegitimate son may have easily been one of the reasons which prompted him to leave Sydney in 1861 and make a new home in Grafton where no one knew him.

Whatever the truth may be, we have a clear picture of a solitary, lonely, morbidly introspective man, with a business declining from indifference or neglect, suffering from unknown and possibly imaginary guilt aggravated by ill-health. We know from the evidence given at the inquest that at Christmas 1867, before leaving Grafton for a short holiday at Clarence Heads, he had written a letter to Mr Stevenson, his closest friend, and left it in the care of his house-keeper, Mrs Wakefield, with instructions to forward the letter to Mr Stevenson "if anything happened to him". The letter read:

> My Dear Stevenson,—I leave this in the hands of Mrs Wakefield, in case anything should happen to me. I have left you my executor, and my will is in my desk in my office. I am sure you will accept this trust, and do me justice. . . . My desire is that my poor boy should be sent to my father in England, who would bring him up as a gentleman. . . . To enable you to carry out this, and to leave him in charge of some person till you can send him home, I have made you his guardian. Praying you (in case of accident) to fulfill these wishes for me,
>
> I am, yours etc
>
> James L. Michael.
>
> Christmas, 1867.

In his apologia Sheridan Moore, who was anxious to refute the suspicion of suicide, maintained that Michael had written this letter because he was ill at the time and feared he might die of natural causes. But his doctor claimed that he was suffering "from simple fever with gastric derangement". I find the words "in case of accident" significant; a sick man would surely write "in the event of my death".

Michael was to suffer one more blow in the few months left to him before his death. In April he brought an action in the District Court against a certain George Morris of South Grafton to recover the sum of £26 9s. 11d. for professional services. When the case was heard Morris produced a telegram from another solicitor, a Mr Macalister of Brisbane, to the effect that Michael had received certain moneys on his

(Morris's) account which Michael had not accounted for. Michael claimed that this was untrue, that the name of Morris in the telegram had been mistaken for "Maurice", and that nothing had been recovered at the suit of Morris against Hutchins. In spite of this the Judge (Judge Meymott) found for Morris against Michael and the case was dismissed. In fact the judge was wrong. After Michael's death Mr Macalister wrote a letter to the editor of the *Empire* on 27th May pointing out that Michael's evidence had been correct, that the telegram had referred to "Maurice" not Morris, and that the error had been made by a clerk who was ignorant of the transaction. Mr Macalister ended his letter with the words: "In justice to the memory of the deceased gentleman, I think it but right that his probity should be vindicated."

Unfortunately this vindication came too late for James Michael. Quite apart from the loss of the money, which was serious enough to a man who was already in some financial difficulties, Michael felt keenly the injustice of the verdict which, as he was heard "repeatedly to say", stamped him as a dishonest man. If one accepts that Michael committed suicide, then plainly this verdict may have been the last straw in deciding him to take his life a fortnight later.

We can recount the last few hours of Michael's life in some detail. About 6 p.m. on Sunday, 28th April, his clerk, William Robertson, called at his house in Victoria Street about some business letters which were to go by the mail steamer which left Grafton for Sydney the following morning. He found him "in his usual health and spirits". When the clerk had gone Michael decided to go for a walk and asked his housekeeper, Mrs Wakefield, to bring him his galoshes—pathetic touch!—and his pipe. He then left the house, saying he would not be long. Mrs Wakefield too said that Michael had been "unusually cheerful" both on the Saturday and Sunday. About 7 p.m. Michael Tierney, a constable in the Grafton police force, met him in Victoria Street coming from his house. The constable wished him "Good evening" and Michael replied.

Victoria Street must then have been very similar to what it is today. It is a pretty road which runs along the bank of the

Clarence though today the river is hidden by the grassy bank of the levee. One or two of the present houses must indeed have been there in Michael's day. As you go westwards, going upstream, the Clarence takes a great bend and the road peters out into an inviting path along the river bank. It must have been this path which Michael took. It was about sunset and I like to think that he could see the dark blue of the New England Range against the pale colours of the evening sky.

Michael never returned. After a time Mrs Wakefield reported his absence to the police. She also went into his private room—also described as his "microscopic room"—where she found this poem on the lid of a small box on the table. Ironically, it was the best poem Michael ever wrote.

> What songs were they the Sirens sung?
>   What name was that Achilles bore,
> When young and fair, the maids among,
>   A maiden's dress and mien he wore?
> I cannot tell—yet thought is free,
>   Some guess, perchance, might answer well;
> But after death what shall we be
>   Ah! that indeed I cannot tell.
>
> Who lives as I have had to live,
>   Misjudged by all, without a friend;
> Will little fear the alternative,
>   To die, to die, and there an end.
> Ah me, it is not death we fear,
>   When griefs are more than we can bear,
> But if we are not happy here
>   Who knows? We shall be quiet THERE.
>
> Truly my trial has been sore,
>   In sorrow have I woke and slept,
> And held a face of calm before
>   The world, that guessed not that I wept.
> And yet somewhere, somehow, I know
>   There must be mercy yet for me;
> Man will have none for me below—
>   My Father! I will go to Thee.

That should be the end of the story. This poem, together with the letter to Mr Stevenson, seems the clearest proof of intended suicide. Yet there is one last mystery to raise some doubts. At the inquest the doctor, Robert Purdie, confirmed what the farmer had noticed: although the general appearance of the body indicated that death had been caused by drowning, the right eye had been severely injured, "the wound being jagged and such as might be produced from falling on a broken bottle, or inflicted by a blow from a switch; the frontal bone of the orbit was broken by the force of the blow; the injuries were such as would be more likely to be produced from falling on something than from a blow; the injury to the right eye had evidently been inflicted only a very short time previous to death."

This rather confused evidence seems to leave open a number of possibilities. Was Michael's death an accident, and if so, how? Was it murder, and if so, who? Murder seems the least likely and I find it almost impossible to believe. Sheridan Moore said that Michael had made some enemies in the district during his last years at Grafton, but who has not? One would require very much more substantial evidence to believe that someone had waylayed Michael on the riverbank, struck him a blow with a stick and then tumbled him into the river. Yet one must admit that this hypothesis is conceivable.

Then was it an accident? To believe this one must accept that Michael had fallen so heavily on some object—perhaps a broken bottle—that he had been temporarily stunned and fallen into the river. Once again it is possible, but not very likely.

On the other hand those who believe that Michael took his own life also have some difficult questions to answer. One can argue, for instance, that a man who is contemplating suicide does not usually call for his pipe and galoshes. But then he might not have decided on suicide when he left the house but only when he found himself standing on the river bank. It may also be asked why Michael, an amateur chemist who fifteen years before had urged the advantages of Prussic acid, should have chosen the rather difficult and clumsy method of death by drowning—especially if it is true, as

Sheridan Moore said, that he had a morbid fear of the water. However men do not always behave rationally, especially in moments of desperation. I am also sceptical of Michael's alleged hydrophobia. He had a boathouse and therefore, presumably, a boat. He was also fond of the sea. The galoshes merely prove that he disliked getting his feet wet—a very different thing. We may also dismiss Sheridan Moore's argument that Michael could not have committed suicide since he was a devout Christian though not a church-goer. Christians have taken their own lives before now, even though it is considered to be a mortal sin. Indeed a firm belief in an after life may be an added inducement.

But there is still one major difficulty. If Michael in fact committed suicide, how did he receive the blow over his right eye which, the doctor said, occurred *before* death by drowning? Well, the doctor may have been wrong. One doubts whether Doctor Purdie would have had much experience in forensic science. It seems to me at least possible that Michael's body was struck while floating in the river after his death, perhaps by some cheerful farmer rowing home in the dark after an evening in Grafton's hotel. He would have felt only a soft bump.

However the doubts were sufficient to persuade the jury to bring in an open verdict and I can see no evidence strong enough to reverse their decision now. All we can say with certainty is that Michael wished to die and that he did die some time on the evening of 28th April 1868. Kendall, who visited the grave and wrote a moving poem on his death, left a note saying that "Michael is buried in a lovely spot on the north bank of the Clarence River which had been a favourite haunt of the poet." The Grafton Historical Society claims that he was buried in the Grafton Cemetery which is certainly on the north bank of the Clarence though about two miles from the river and, to be honest, not particularly beautiful. It also claims that he wrote the inscription for his own headstone but, strangely, does not seem to have recorded it. The last time I was in Grafton I consulted the Clerk of Petty Sessions, who is also the Registrar of Births, Marriages and Deaths, the Municipal Council, which is now the trustee of the cemetery, and the oldest undertakers in Grafton without success. None of them knew anything of Michael or could tell me where he is buried.

Perhaps the grave no longer exists. On a fine afternoon in August I went out to the cemetery to see if I could find it for myself. There were many old graves of Highlanders—McPhersons, Camerons, and Robertsons—and many of Germans —Schwinghammers, Kleindiensts and others—in that sad, untidy cemetery on the river flats which stretch to the north of the town. Some of them too had died by accident in the Big River. But I could not find Michael's tomb, though Kendall's words were accurate enough:

> Soft surprises of the sun—*
> Swift, serene—
> O'er the mute grave-grasses run,
> Cold and green.

Perhaps a man who, however unhappy during his lifetime, is fortunate enough to have such a moving tribute paid to him by another poet does not require any other memorial. But it seems to me that James Lionel Michael was of sufficient interest in his own right for Grafton to mark his grave in some more fitting manner.

---

* James McAuley, who first drew my attention to Michael, has taken the first line of this fine verse as the title for one of his own collections of poetry.